# A New Beginning for Pastors and Congregations

# A New Beginning for Pastors and Congregations

## Building an Excellent Match Upon Your Shared Strengths

Kennon L. Callahan

Jossey-Bass
San Francisco

Unless otherwise stated, biblical quotations are from *The Holy Bible, Revised Standard Version* (copyright © Thomas Nelson & Sons). Also cited are the *King James Version* and *New English Bible* (K J V and NEB: Copyright © Christianity Today, Inc., 1965) and *New American Standard Bible* (NASB: Copyright © The Lockman Foundation, 1960, 1962, 1963, 1968, 1971, 1973).

Jossey-Bass books and products are available through most bookstores. To contact Jossey-Bass directly, call (888) 378-2537, fax to (800) 605-2665, or visit our website at www.josseybass.com.

Substantial discounts on bulk quantities of Jossey-Bass books are available to corporations, professional associations, and other organizations. For details and discount information, contact the special sales department at Jossey-Bass.

TCF Manufactured in the United States of America on Lyons Falls Turin Book. This paper is acid-free and 100 percent totally chlorine-free.

**Library of Congress Cataloging-in-Publication Data**

Callahan, Kennon L.
  A new beginning for pastors and congregations: building an excellent match upon your shared strengths / Kennon L. Callahan. —1st ed.
    p. cm.
  Includes index.
  ISBN 0-7879-4289-8 (alk. paper)
  1. Pastoral theology.  I. Title.
  BV4011 .C28 1999
  253—dc21                                                      99-6345

FIRST EDITION
*HB Printing*        10 9 8 7 6 5 4 3 2 1

# Contents

97704

*To Dan, Lynne, Nancy, and Valerie*
*Who are a blessing in our lives,*
*And with whom we share New Beginnings*
*As we head into the New Millennium*
*Together.*

Kennon L. and Julia McCoy Callahan

# Preface

This book is for pastors and congregations who look forward to a new beginning. Congregations and pastors will benefit in developing an excellent match with one another, building upon their mutual, shared strengths. Four relationships between pastors and congregations will benefit:

1. *A new beginning.* The pastor and congregation come together for the first time. Each year, many pastors and congregations discover one another for the first time. They want a healthy, strong beginning.

2. *A second new beginning.* The pastor and congregation are doing fine and having fun. They have been together for some time. They decide they want to move their relationship to an even deeper, richer, stronger level.

3. *A restart, from a positive first beginning.* The initial start between the pastor and the congregation was fine. It went well. However, they hit some troubled times and rough, painful patches. They want to restart together.

4. *A restart, from a weak first beginning.* The initial start between the pastor and the congregation did not go well. Things have not been going well since. There has been pain, stress, and distress. The pastor and the congregation decide they want a new start together.

Each year, many pastors and congregations discover one another for the first time. Many rediscover one another with a fresh, new spirit. They want a healthy, strong relationship with one another.

God gives us a remarkable gift. God gives us the gift of a new beginning. This is true for both a new start and a restart. Have fun with the book. Have fun with the new beginning God is giving you.

# Acknowledgments

I want to thank the countless congregations and pastors who have been kind enough to share with me their insights and experiences of new beginnings together. Their common journeys are remarkable, and I am continually amazed at the generosity and wisdom with which they share their lives together in God's mission.

I want to thank Julie McCoy Callahan for her wisdom and insight in developing this new book. Her suggestions have been very helpful. Most especially, I thank her for the many remarkable new beginnings we have shared together. We met in high school, became good friends, began to date, fell in love, married, and have shared together in an amazing array of wonderful new beginnings across the years. Her graciousness and generosity, her gentle wisdom and deep love are extraordinary gifts and blessings in our lives together.

I want to thank Sarah Polster. She is a most remarkable editor. This is our third book together. I am grateful for her many contributions to this work. She has a remarkable sense of clarity. Her understanding of the material is exceptional. Her suggestions have advanced the book considerably. It is a stronger, more helpful book because of her wisdom.

I want to thank Joanne Clapp Fullagar. She and her team have done excellent work in bringing this book into being. I am grateful for her helpfulness and her thoughtfulness. The whole production staff at Jossey-Bass is a remarkable group. I am grateful for Joanne's work, and for her attention to detail. The production of this book has moved forward in a straightforward, timely way because of her leadership.

I encourage you to enjoy the book. You will find it a good fun book. The wisdom and suggestions will benefit you. May God bless the new beginnings in your life.

KENNON L. CALLAHAN
*July 1999*

# 1

# Beginning the First Day

Tom became a legend. Sometimes, in quiet moments of reflection, people still talk about the event, even as many years have come and gone.

He walked into the waiting room at seven o'clock on a Friday morning. The family gathered there did not know him. He did not know them. He simply walked in and said gently, "I've come to wait with you." With that one act, with those few words, the legend began.

They were not expecting him. They could hardly imagine that *he* had come to be with *them*. Yet with their worry and their growing grief, they welcomed him. They were glad he was there with them. Their relief, their joy at his presence was much like that experienced by farmers and ranchers who welcome the rains of life after a drought.

The waiting room was quiet, deathly so. They were waiting out the results of the surgery, wrapped in their own thoughts. No one spoke. Thinking of the good times they had shared, and of the other times they could have shared if they hadn't been so busy. Three hours, they were told—they should know something by ten o'clock.

The family could hardly believe they were there, in that hospital, in that waiting room, with its old magazines and sterile smells. Events happen so swiftly. Mrs. O'Hara saw her doctor Tuesday for a routine matter. Test results came back late Wednesday afternoon. She was admitted to the hospital Thursday. Surgery was scheduled for seven o'clock Friday morning. This was not a casual elective procedure.

Tom stayed with the family during the hours of surgery. There were moments of quiet conversation. There were times of silence. His simple presence brought confidence and assurance. He stood up as they did when the doctor came in, still in his scrubs, to report good news to the family. Mrs. O'Hara was in the recovery room. The operation was successful. She would return to their midst and recover her health. Naturally and gently, Tom led the family in brief prayers of joy and thanksgiving.

Tom had just moved into the parsonage the day before. The old, yellowed moving van rolled up to the door Thursday morning. The movers—one old codger who had done more moving than most folks would in four lifetimes, along with two younger men, with eagerness and muscle—carried the many boxes into the house. Tom's wife pointed the movers to the various rooms where certain boxes belonged. There was much unpacking to be done.

That moving day, Tom and Mary had all they could say grace over: directing the movers; helping the three children, with their innate excitement and enthusiasm, their desire to explore the house and the neighborhood; opening the boxes marked to be unpacked first, finding the essentials to begin setting up the house and living in it.

There were the pleasant moments of greeting as people from the congregation dropped by to welcome them. One couple, Paul and Ann, brought a homemade cherry pie (when Tom and his family ate it later that night, they agreed it was the best they had ever tasted). An older woman, Mrs. Merrill, who lived just up the road brought apples, strawberries, and bananas, saying the fruit would tide them over until they could do some shopping. The strawberries were freshly picked from her patch. Another couple, Don and Linda, brought milk and freshly baked bread, still warm from the oven. Others came to welcome them. It was a full, eventful afternoon, with much warmth and busyness, expectancy and hard work.

In one of the conversations (Tom could not quite remember later which one, and finally it did not really matter), he learned, almost accidentally, of Mrs. O'Hara's surgery the next morning.

Mrs. O'Hara was not a member of his new congregation. She lived a simple, quiet life in a nearby small town. Her church, if she had one, would have been in that town. Most thought she did not have a church. Tom learned later that Mr. O'Hara had died several years before, after a long, painful illness. In the days and years following his death, she had spent her time loving and helping her family—her two sisters and one brother, her nieces and nephews. She was the aunt, loved and respected by her family, some of whom were members, at least formally, of Tom's new congregation. Mostly, they came on Easter, Christmas, and a few other special occasions.

Tom simply went early the next morning to be with the family. He did not think it out. There was no plan. They were part of his congregation. He would go and wait with them.

This simple pastoral act began the legend. By Saturday afternoon, word of Tom's compassionate hospital visit had traveled throughout the congregation. The grapevine worked well that Friday and Saturday. This was good news. It traveled fast.

A second simple act happened on Sunday morning. At the beginning of the sermon, Tom introduced Mary and their three children, saying that they all came to be family with them. He looked forward to getting to know them, richly and fully. Then he said, "On the table in the narthex, you will find three sheets of paper, one for each of the coming three weeks. You are welcome to sign up so we can visit together. I have set aside fifteen time slots during each week—there are times for lunch, morning coffee, afternoon coffee, breakfast, five o'clock, or evening—pick one of the times that works for you. I will come to your place of work, or your home, or wherever you suggest. I really look forward to our getting to know one another as friends and family."

People signed up, with some amazement and wonder. This had not happened in recent memory.

The three weeks came and went. The congregation members got to know Tom personally. He got to know them personally. Mostly, they discovered that Tom would listen to them. He actually wanted to know about them. He was not brimming over with plans for the church or personal advice. He was interested in them—as people.

The previous pastor was there three years. Actually, he was only "passin' through." He never completely unpacked. Some boxes, yes; just enough to get by. He saw this congregation as a stepping stone to a bigger church. He needed to put in his time here in order to get to where he wanted to be. He never really participated in the community. He never really unpacked his mind or opened his heart. He was simply moving through.

The pastor before him was there for seven years. He came at the age of fifty-nine. For the first three years, he gave some time to the congregation. Then he began planning his retirement home some distance away. The next four years, his mind and heart focused mostly on that project. Some people said he really retired when he first came to the church.

Before that, the previous pastor was there for five years. Much of his time was spent in front of his computer. No one seemed to know what he was doing with all that computer time. This was not a large congregation. There were about forty-five active families in regular attendance. There were not enough families to justify so much time spent keeping so few church records up to date on a computer.

Over time, it became apparent that he was simply not interested in being there. He was putting in time. It was not that he wanted to be in a bigger church. It was not that he had longings to move up the ladder. The congregation had welcomed him, warmly and generously. It was a healthy, loving congregation. He appreciated them and was grateful for their interest in him. He was simply not certain where he wanted to be. Finally, in the fifth year, he moved on.

Across those previous fifteen years, the pastors did minimal visiting, caring, and shepherding. Although they were decent enough, they did not really love the people. They put in their time, the barest time. Some people later had trouble remembering their names.

Fifteen years of drought ended. With Tom, the rains came. Gently and steadily, the life-giving rains of sharing and caring, loving and shepherding began. Like dormant flowers in a desert, people awakened to Tom's quiet, rich, full compassion.

Many years have come and gone. Tom and Mary's oldest son is now in medical school. Their daughter is in her senior year of college, headed to a master's degree and then to teaching. Their youngest son is a sophomore in college, looking forward to seminary and thence to serving as a pastor with congregations.

Tom and Mary have aged some. They have enjoyed some of the happiest years of their lives. There have been struggles along the way; yet these have seemed minor compared to the good times they have shared. They have watched their children grow into whole, healthy adults. Their oldest will be married next year. Their daughter is happily busy with her friends and schooling. There are several boys in her life, but no one special as yet—well, maybe one possibility. There is plenty of time.

Their youngest is having fun. It was on a mission trip between his freshman and sophomore years in college that his calling to the ministry became clear to him. He is thrilled by the joy of his discovery. His schooling has taken on richer, more profound meaning. He is at peace with where he is headed. Tom and Mary look with wonder across the years and are grateful they are so richly blessed. Their congregation is whole and healthy, strong and vibrant.

## A First Impression

Tom's ministry is legendary. With a slender build, he is of average height. His manner is quiet and unassuming. His walk is steady and purposeful. His clothes are plain and simple. His shy smile breaks gradually on his face like a new dawn. He is amiable and kindhearted. He enjoys people, and across the years people have enjoyed sharing with him. His spirit is gentle and gracious.

He lives a life of compassion and wisdom, integrity and honesty. He is a good shepherd; a helpful preacher; a wise, caring leader; and a community pastor. People look to him as a caring, helpful person. He never planned it, yet he is a legend in the community in which he lives. The legend began with those two simple, generous, gracious acts in the first three days of being their pastor.

Your first three days shape the first three weeks. You can never make a first impression the second time. The first three weeks shape the first three months. How you as pastor use this time together with your congregation shapes the first three years. How you begin shapes how you continue and where you end.

We begin the first day. Regrettably, a few pastors have the notion, as they move into a new calling, a new settlement, a new appointment, that they can take a week or two to get everything organized and then begin. They spend these important first days organizing the office, unpacking all of their books, and getting their desks in order. Sadly, they lose the best first days of their ministry with their new congregation.

We only get the first days one time. How we begin in the first, second, and third days shapes where we head together in the first, second, and third week. By then, we have shaped where we are headed in the first, second, and third month. At the end of the third month, our direction for the first three years is in place.

In the first few days and weeks, you and your congregation teach one another who you plan to be together. Many pastors, in these early days, constructively teach their congregation that they plan to be a good shepherd, a helpful preacher, a wise and caring leader, a community pastor. Many congregations participate in helping this constructive beginning to grow forward. They teach their new pastor, and teach one another, that they plan to shepherd persons, worship and pray, be wise and caring leaders, and serve well the community in mission.

There is some sense in which you begin your relationship with your new congregation during the interview with the personnel committee before you even move into the community. The committee members develop a first impression of you in that beginning interview. So do you—of them. You describe your immediate impression to friends and family, colleagues, and denominational leaders. They do the same—with their friends, family, leaders, grassroots members, and persons in the community.

You may visit the community one or more times, driving around to see what you think. This is sometimes done with a guide from the congregation, or incognito, or both. You are further developing your impression of the congregation and the community. In some instances, you may have one or more meetings with a wider group than the personnel committee, and even with the congregation as a whole.

These are exploratory gatherings. The impressions gained thereby are *beginning* impressions. They are tentative, preliminary in nature. There is not yet a final decision by either you or the congregation as to whether it makes sense for you and this congregation to live together and share and work together in God's mission.

You make your first *lasting* impression on the congregation and the community as you move in. The congregation and the community make a similar impression on you as they welcome their new pastor.

How we welcome one another shapes how we live together. How we begin shapes how we live and share together. It is not "we move in, get organized for the first several weeks and then, after everything is in order, we begin." We begin as we move in. It is not as if we can call a time out, move in, somehow get settled, and then really begin our ministry a few days or weeks later. We begin the first day.

The word goes out to the community grapevine as you move in. You are making your first impression as the movers carry your belongings into your new home. Across the years, people have shared with me the stories of what happened and what did not happen in the first few days. With the congregation as a whole, particularly the grassroots members, and the community at large, the first impression begins that first day.

# What Makes an Excellent Match?

An excellent match develops between a pastor and a congregation when the two resonate with one another. It is not that the match is immediately, fully in place. Rather, the basic resonance is present in four preliminary ways. Over time, the pastor and congregation develop these four more richly and fully.

## Falling in Love

First, the pastor and the people fall in love with each other. They develop a healthy, constructive relationship of trust, respect, appreciation, and genuine love with one another. Regrettably, a few pastors—and, truth be known, a few congregations—want a codependent-dependent relationship with one another. Sadly, they seek an unhealthy relationship of the type that is frequently born out of low self-esteem, a compulsion toward perfectionism, wishful thinking, and the illusion that doing more is a sign of being helpful.

To avoid this unhealthy pattern of behavior, a few pastors choose to maintain only a "professional relationship" with their congregation, keeping the congregation at a distance. They may even have been taught to never make friends with anyone in the congregation, to avoid any show of favoritism. Regrettably, they miss the deep, rich, full relationships with their congregation that make life worth living. Distance begets distance. Love begets love.

Likewise, a few congregations, burned by an unhealthy codependent-dependent relationship with a former pastor, determine to keep the new pastor at a distance. One pastor and congregation that I know had such a dependent relationship. Both the pastor's low self-esteem and that of the congregation were fed by the nature of the relationship. But dependent relationships require enormous energy to be sustained.

Finally worn out by trying to sustain his part of the un-healthiness, the pastor suddenly, abruptly left. The congregation felt betrayed, angry, disillusioned. Determined not to be burned again, they decided, informally and almost without realizing they had done so, to keep the next pastor at bay. But the solution to an unhealthy relationship of codependency is not to move to the other extreme and have no relationship.

A healthy relationship is born out of solid self-esteem. There is mutual trust and respect. Progress, not perfectionism, is how life is lived, one day at a time. There are realistic and achievable expectancies for the relationship. Both the pastor and the congregation share help with one another.

Giving "more" help is not a sign of being helpful. More is always one more over the horizon. We can never achieve more. It sets up a never-ending horizon of failure. It creates a frustrating, never-ending codependent relationship. Such relationships are cruel, not kind, precisely because they suppress the latent strengths present in the relationship and cause people to stifle their own self-reliance and self-sufficiency, their own inner resources to be helpful to themselves.

Jesus told a parable that illustrates the spirit of healthy helping. The Samaritan binds up the wounds of the man he finds in the ditch, beaten and robbed, and sees that he gets to the nearby inn. The innkeeper then delivers just enough help so that the man can be on his way. There is nothing in the parable to suggest that the innkeeper delivered so much help that the man, in appreciation and gratitude, lived, lo, the rest of his days with the innkeeper.

In healthy helpfulness, the helping person delivers just enough help to be helpful but not so much help that the help becomes harmful and creates a pattern of codependency. The Samaritan and the innkeeper do just enough so that the man can continue his journey. God shares help with us in this spirit. God delivers sufficient help for the day at hand, so that, in whole and healthy ways, we can resume the journey of this life.

When a pastor and people fall in love with one another, they develop a healthy relationship of mutual helping. They discover rich, full compassion with one another, born of mutual trust and respect. They live with the desire to nurture a whole, healthy life together with the grace of God.

## A Good Fit

The second factor that contributes to an excellent match is meshing the pastor's competencies with the objectives and hopes of the congregation and the congregation's mission in the community. Examples abound of a pastor's competencies not meshing with a congregation's objectives, hopes, and mission. I remember having dinner with a pastor one evening in a wonderful restaurant. It was an excellent meal; now we were discussing his future. He had been with his congregation for four turbulent, upsetting years. There were lulls in the fighting, truces, and resting up for the next fight. There were times of calm and peace, but mutual animosities were persistent.

After our dinner, we were walking across the parking lot to his car when he asked me a question that was lying heavily on his heart: "Dr. Callahan, do you think I should move on?" I responded, gently and quietly, "Yes," and kept on walking toward his car.

He stopped and asked me what I meant. I said:

> As I have listened, you have taught me this. You are an excellent passing quarterback, and you are working with an excellent running team. They are going to win games, and they are going to do it on the ground three and four yards per play. But you keep calling these forty-yard, down-and-out passing patterns, and there is no one out there to catch the ball.

Two possibilities occur to me. Either you can change—learn how to be a ground-game quarterback—or you can move on to a congregation that knows how to do a passing game.

What is happening is that you are blaming them and you are blaming yourself. They are blaming you and blaming themselves. There is no "fault" here. The biblical principle teaches us that there is a diversity of gifts. With honor and integrity, you have certain gifts. They have certain gifts. They simply do not mesh together.

Fortunately, many pastors and congregations learn how to mesh the pastor's competencies and objectives and those of the congregation. Frequently, they bridge their strengths and objectives to discover a mutually advantageous way forward. In doing so, the competencies, objectives, and hopes of both the pastor and the congregation live themselves out in the congregation's mission in the community.

## Mutual Growth

The third way in which the pastor and the people resonate well together is if they are mutually growing in the mission. This may not necessarily mean the church is immediately growing in the number of new members. Mission growth is different from—and more helpful than—church growth. Mission growth has to do with the persons we are serving in mission in the wider community—helping them with their lives and destinies in the name of Christ.

In the mission growth movement, the compelling question is, "Who is our mission?" That is, "Who is God inviting us to serve in mission?" God invites us to a theology of service, not a theology of survival. God invites us to a theology of mission, not a theology of maintenance. God plants around us people with whom we can be constructively in mission.

Healthy congregations discover a specific concrete missional objective. They may have more than one. The point is that they only need to find one specific mission to strengthen an excellent match between the pastor and the congregation. They share concrete, effective help, not simply glowing generalities or good intentions. People are genuinely helped. The happy by-product of this mission is that the pastor and the congregation grow and develop an even richer, fuller match with each other.

Some congregations share concrete, effective help with a specific human hurt and hope, such as addiction, grief, loneliness, or fear. Some share handles of help and hope with individual persons and families as they move through specific life stages. For example, some congregations are exceptionally helpful with the preschool and elementary school life stages. Some help people who are wrestling with midlife crisis, or experiencing early retirement. Some congregations advance a constructive presence with specific community concerns and interests such as education, safety, or poverty. Whatever the mission, they live beyond themselves.

On the other hand, people who are preoccupied with themselves have difficulty developing healthy relationships with those around them. To some extent, the church growth question of "Do you want your church to grow?" is a self-serving focus. Pastors and congregations who have become preoccupied with their own survival are focused on themselves. On the surface, the pastor and the congregation seem to have a mutual sense of direction. Both appear to have an interest in growing their church. Ironically, this self-centered focus diminishes the possibility of a match between the pastor and the congregation.

People who live beyond themselves discover both their own best true selves and the best true selves of those around them. People who share in mission develop a match. They discover a mutual cause beyond themselves and, in doing so, find one another. Their mutuality and generosity toward those with whom they are in mission helps them share mutuality and generosity among one another.

I remember a congregation that had been dying slowly over a quarter of a century. As each year passed, there were fewer people in worship. Giving declined. As people passed on, the membership gradually diminished. Somewhere on the way down, they became preoccupied with their decline. They adopted an objective of church growth, hoping to stem the decline. They continued to decline. People are not drawn to a group preoccupied with its own decline.

Over the years, they blamed themselves and they blamed the succession of pastors for their decline. There were no excellent matches between the pastors and the congregation across those years. Then a pastor came to them whose longings were in mission growth. He helped them discover a mission with elementary children and their families in the nearby elementary schools.

They found two ways to live out their mission. First, they shared the most helpful, competent vacation Bible school in the area. Second, they developed the best after-school program in the community. Their spirit was expressed as: "Whether we continue to decline or not is beside the point. We plan to help these kids and their families, whether they come to our church or not."

Blessed with their newfound mission, a healthy relationship began to emerge between the pastor and the congregation. People who are helping other people get along with one another better.

## Growing Whole and Healthy Lives

The fourth factor that contributes to an excellent match is if the pastor and the people are growing whole, healthy lives together. They are experiencing the grace of God, the compassion of Christ, and the healing hope of the Holy Spirit. They are advancing the gifts and competencies with which God is blessing them.

Healthy people develop healthy congregations. Healthy congregations develop healthy people. The two go hand in hand. If the pastor is growing a whole, healthy life in his own being, this encourages people in the congregation to advance their lives as well. The reverse is also true. If several people in a congregation are growing and developing the health of their lives, it encourages a pastor to grow as well.

While serving one congregation, a particular pastor finally discovered his strengths for living a healthy life. In his early life and while growing up, he had been taught to focus on his weaknesses. This perspective continued with stern rigor, with quiet determination, into his adult life. That was how he dealt with his congregation: he helped them focus on their weaknesses and shortcomings as a congregation. This in turn created and reinforced people who in their own lives focused on their weaknesses and shortcomings. The downhill spiral continued. People are not drawn to groups that are preoccupied with their problems.

This pastor was participating in one of my seminars when I shared with the group the insight that people who claim their strengths claim God, claim God's gifts. People who deny their strengths deny God, deny God's gifts. I went on to suggest that when we begin with our weaknesses we are in the weakest position to tackle our weaknesses. When we begin with our strengths—God's gifts—and build on our strengths, we are in the strongest position to tackle our weaknesses and shortcomings.

The pastor went home from the seminar with a new perspective, a new way of thinking. He began to focus on his gifts, strengths, and competencies. This gave people in the congregation encouragement to do likewise in their own lives.

Together, pastor and people, they began to do the same with their congregation. People who are growing in their own lives have a healthier likelihood of developing an excellent match as pastor and congregation.

God gives us new beginnings. Across the course of our lives, we are blessed by God with new beginnings that give us the chance to grow and develop. For some of us, these are early new beginnings while we are young, with the dawning of our lives before us. Others of us think life is about half over, and all we have to do is stay out of major trouble 'til the end; to our amazement, God comes to us and gives us a new day. For all of us, God continuously invites us to new life.

We are coming to the beginnings of the third millennium, the start of the twenty-first century. These are remarkable turning points in human civilization. Many celebrations will occur, with good fun and good times. Much joy and enthusiasm will be shared. Many projections about the future will be put forth.

These are the elements of any new beginning. There is a sense of expectancy. Our spirits are high. With wonder and joy, enthusiasm and anticipation, we look forward to the days and years to come. There is some doubt, some uncertainty. We are not always sure life will work out as well as we hope. Nevertheless, we look forward to a new beginning. We renew ourselves. We discover new possibilities. We grow in our understanding of life. We advance the strengths and competencies God gives us.

Pastors and congregations create excellent matches together. This is true of both a new start and a restart. The suggestions in the following chapters help you develop a new beginning. The relationships between pastor and congregation will be richer and stronger, deeper and more helpful.

# 2

# Growing Excellent Matches

S ome beginning matches of pastors and congregations can be recognized as excellent matches from the first day. Everyone worked well in the search for the new pastor—with wisdom and judgment, vision and compassion, common sense and prayer—to achieve an excellent match. They knew from early on that this was an excellent match. From the beginning, they resonated well together in the four ways discussed in Chapter One. They began to love one another. The competencies of the pastor and of the congregation reinforced one another. They began to discover a mutual mission together. They are growing whole, healthy lives together.

Regrettably, some matches are what I call excellent mismatches from the first day. No one intends to create a mismatch. Indeed, everyone works hard to avoid this predicament. Yet, for whatever reasons, sometimes it happens. We see, early on, that there is no resonance, no likelihood for an excellent match.

Sometimes, I think, the harder a pastor, a congregation, and a denominational leader work to avoid creating a mismatch, the more likely it is to slip through. We get too tense and tight, nervous and anxious. We forget the many solid matches that grow and develop. We remember the mismatches that have happened.

We become too anxious that everything must work really well, almost exactly and perfectly, from the first minute. We do not give ourselves, as pastor and congregation, time to grow and develop together. Instead, what happens is that our old friend, compulsion toward perfectionism, shows up. We try too hard. We are not relaxed. The result is that we head toward an excellent mismatch.

Most matches are somewhere in the middle. They are neither immediate excellent matches nor obvious mismatches. They are possibilities that can go either way.

Overall, there are more immediate excellent matches than there are excellent *mis*matches. The excellent matches are constructively off and running. What helps is for us to deliver the gift of encouragement to these beginning excellent matches. However, regrettably, we often become preoccupied with the excellent mismatches. Amid much noise and confusion, we allow them to take up considerable time. Denominational leaders are called in to adjudicate and referee, console and consult. Community grapevines feed on them.

All this attention creates the illusion that there are more excellent mismatches than really exist. In reality, there are more excellent matches. Moreover, the majority of calling and appointive matches are neither immediate excellent matches nor excellent mismatches. The majority of matches are in the middle; they have the possibility of moving one way or the other. The best contribution of calling and appointive processes is to create this constructive *possibility*. With this possibility, the responsibility lies with the pastor and congregation to move forward to develop a healthy, excellent match.

At their best, calling and appointive processes primarily seek to create this possibility. They have done solid work when, as in the vast majority of openings, they accomplish this. Whenever denominational leaders place upon themselves the burden that they *must* create an excellent match, they are laying too much upon themselves. Further, the effort takes away from the pastor's and congregation's ownership for developing together an excellent match.

*Ownership* is key. It is the task of the pastor and the congregation, given an excellent possibility, to grow and develop—with one another—an excellent match. It is not the task of the denomination to deliver the excellent match. Even if the denomination could do so, the pastor and the congregation would have no ownership for that excellent match.

It is decisive that the pastor and the congregation participate together in growing a healthy, excellent match. When we begin well together, by investing wisely in the first three days, three weeks, and three months, we move forward, we grow and develop an excellent match—and we have ownership for the match we are achieving together.

## Current Matches

Some pastors and congregations are off to a good start, and would like this good start to be even stronger. Some may be off to a weak start and would like to have a new first year. Some pastors and congregations are in their third, fourth, or fifth year together and would like to develop an even richer, fuller relationship together. Some are in their sixth, seventh, or eighth year and would like to try a new start, a new chapter, with each other.

You can grow forward an excellent match in your early time together. Further, you can grow a richer, deeper excellent match whenever you would like to make a new start with your current congregation. Some pastors, wanting a new start, think the primary way forward is to move on to a new church and thereby have a new beginning. But you can have "a second pastorate," that is, a new start, a new pastorate, in your present congregation.

Over the years, I have discovered two helpful insights that I share with pastors and congregations.

First, I encourage pastors to know that their next best congregation is likely the one they have now, as they help their congregation grow and develop in the grace of God.

Second, I encourage congregations to know that their next best pastor is likely the one they have now, as they help their pastor grow and develop in the grace of God.

Certainly, there are exceptions to both insights.

With respect to the first insight, I encourage pastors to know that there are not that many plums out there any more. Sometimes, a pastor moves to a congregation only to discover that it *was* a plum—twenty years ago. It is now a hollow shell of its former glory. The pastor discovers there is as much to be done as there was in the congregation he left, if not more.

This is a mission field. This is not a churched culture, where we could count on social conformity to deliver people to the church. The prize congregations of the 1940s and 1950s are mostly gone. In our time, most pastors and congregations are discovering the fresh, new possibilities of an age of mission.

I encourage pastors to know that for the most part there is no point in moving simply because one or two recalcitrant, addictive, abusive, angry, unhealthy persons in their congregation give them a hard time. These people give the same abuse to their own family, and to the rest of the congregation. They have practiced their art for a long time. Further, in a new congregation, we are likely to discover another unhealthy abusive person, simply with a different name and in a different setting.

The way to think through whether it is time to move on is this: consider how you would have fun investing just two years in a congregation. When, as pastor, you leave a congregation, there is an "exit year." You start leaving before you have left. That is, you quit focusing on the long term and focus on the immediate and short term, the here and now. You pack your mind and your heart before you pack your boxes.

Some congregations have become known as four-year churches. Everyone knows that the pastor will be moving on at the end of the fourth year. What happens is that both the pastor and congregation shut down at the end of the third year. Oh, some good things happen in the fourth year, but mostly it is a waiting year until a new pastor comes.

With our new congregation, we have an entry year. Yes, we use the first three months well. We learn and love our new people. Many good things happen. At the same time, in our next congregation it takes us at least a year to begin approaching where we are now with our present congregation. We are looking at two years—an exit year and an entry year. We could use two years of our lives by moving to a new congregation; in some cases, this makes excellent sense.

Alternatively, consider what happens if we use the same two years to develop our present congregation into the congregation to which we might hope to move. In so doing, we move without moving. Sometimes, it makes better sense to take the two-year period and focus on growing and developing together.

We spend less time packing and unpacking boxes, learning streets and stores, places and people. We grow with the people we already know. We develop new strengths and competencies in ourselves and in our congregation. We discover that our next best church is the one we now have as we grow forward together.

To be sure, it is time to move on once you have done solid work. You have grown forward the congregation in its mission to an excellent level. You have done what you set out to do. You now want to have the fun of doing so with a new congregation.

It is time to move on when you sense you have grown competencies in your own ministry as far as you can, in your present setting. You look forward to the freshness of a new setting to advance your growth.

Robert is one of several pastors I offer here as examples of knowing when it is time to move. Robert said to me, "Dr. Callahan, I have been here seven years. It has been a grand time. I feel I have quit growing. I think I need to move on." We talked about several possibilities. We considered the advantages and disadvantages both ways. In Robert's case, for a variety of solid reasons, it made sense for him to move on.

Jack and his congregation were having fun together. They were building a strong, healthy mission. So much so that a plum congregation sought to call Jack away to be their pastor. He looked at where he was with his present congregation, and where he would be in two years by staying with them. He contrasted that with where he would be in two years if he moved to the new congregation. He felt honored that the plum church wanted him. But he stayed.

Harold was enjoying his congregation. Yes, they had some rough times, and one particular conflict still lingered with them. Another congregation expressed interest in his coming to be their pastor. He and his wife thought, talked, and prayed about it. They came to the conclusion that, by moving, they would simply be trading one set of problems for another set of problems. They knew the set of problems with which they were dealing. They decided the pain they were experiencing with their present congregation was not a sufficient reason to move on. They stayed.

Bill was with his congregation for eleven exciting years. It was a roller coaster ride. Bill came there to advance shepherding and worship. He achieved major developments in both. Shepherding teams were flourishing. The new service of worship was helping many. The current service was more stirring and inspiring. The distinctive choirs for each service grew. People were discovering the grace of God in worship.

They had experienced many ups and downs together. Over the years, two major issues nearly divided the congregation. They lived through them. They shared forgiveness and reconciliation. They became closer as pastor and congregation.

In the last four years, the congregation had made a quantum leap in its mission with people in the community. Worship attendance was strong. Giving was generous. Their mission with children and their families in the community were a legend. The hours were long. Bill was tired. Another church hoped he would come and be their pastor. For a fleeting moment, he thought that if he moved he would be less tired, that he would get some rest from the hectic pace.

He stayed. He decided that being tired was not a good reason to move. He was wise enough to see that, if he moved, the pace would still be as hectic, if not more so. He decided to exercise better control over his time, energy, and pace. He finally said, "I might as well learn how to do so here. I am going to have to learn how to lead my life someday, somewhere. I cannot continue to let others do so for me."

For some pastors and congregations, the relationship is going well. They decide to deepen and strengthen it. With some, the relationship has served well, and it is time to move on. Neither being tired nor experiencing problems is in itself a good reason to move on. One considers the wisest use of the two years, and then one makes a healthy decision.

To be sure, when you know it is time to move on, move on. In most settings, you will know the time. When you decide to leave, leave well—with honor and integrity. Bitter words, harsh words, or angry words, if you have any, are better left unsaid. Sad words, grieving words, parting words are helpful, in moderation, without being overdone. Leave with a sense of well-being, with a constructive good-bye.

Most important, you know it is time to move on when you sense that your competencies and the current objectives of the congregation no longer match. Heather has competencies in serving small, strong congregations. She took a weak, declining congregation and over time helped it become a small, strong congregation. She achieved what she has fun doing. It was time to move on.

Phil had the sense that he had done solid work with his congregation. At the same time, he had the feeling he was not growing in his own competencies where he was. He felt drawn to more of a mission setting and a new congregation that would stimulate new growth in him.

Richard served his congregation well. It was an excellent match. Then he discovered a calling to serve on the faculty of a new seminary elsewhere on the planet. His sense of mission now leads him to a new mission field.

For Margaret, a new setting helped her advance her own sense of a whole, healthy life. The rural congregation where she was serving was a solid, healthy congregation. She felt at home, almost, but not quite. But she has more experience living in cities than in open rural country. She moved to an urban congregation. Her rural congregation loved her, and she loved them. But she was wise enough to know that her own personal growth thrives more fully in a city.

Conversely, Iva grew up in the country. She likes the open spaces, where people live fifteen or fifty acres apart, where there is lots of elbow room, and where people still have the fun of being good neighbors. Two-lane roads and modest traffic appeal to her. She likes to see the millions of stars at night, without the reflected glare of city lights. She likes the pace of life in the country, built around the seasons and the harvests. She tried serving a congregation in the city. She did well. The congregation flourished. But her heart is in the country; this is home. Sometimes, it is time to move on.

Sometimes, the way forward is to create a new start where you are. Your next best pastorate may be the one you have now. You can help your congregation grow as you grow. Together, you develop a deeper, richer relationship, a new chapter in your lives in mission.

On occasion, an entire congregation may long for a new pastor. More often, a few people in the congregation become restless to have a new pastor. They feel they have been with their current pastor long enough. Regrettably, their old friend wishful thinking enters the picture. This old friend leads them to believe that out there are vast numbers of pastors who are even better than the present one. They begin to think there are many pastors who have not only all the good attributes of the present pastor but also more competencies in areas where the present pastor has limitations or deficiencies.

The truth is, the pool of available pastors out there is comparatively small. Some people imagine they can find a young pastor with lots of experience. Few pastors have twenty years of experience yet are only thirty-four years old.

Further, among the pastors who are out there are a number still thinking and behaving as though this is a churched culture. They do not seek people out. They spend most of their time inside the church. They wait for people to find the church. Just enough people do so to create the illusion that the long lost churched culture still exists. In our time, a congregation benefits from having a congregational, community, missional pastor, not a professional, churched, cultured pastor.

Yes, there may be a large number of pastors out there, but the truth is they are all human, each with distinctive gifts and distinctive shortcomings. Sometimes, wishful thinking causes us to become restless for a new pastor. Frequently, it is more fun, easier, and more helpful to grow ourselves forward and to help our present pastor grow forward than it is to find a new one.

I encourage congregations to know up front that whenever a pastor leaves, there is the cost of an exit year. Sensing the impending leaving, we leaders (and our congregations) quit looking long-term and starting functioning short-term, day by day, as we grieve the leaving of the current pastor and settle in to get by until the new pastor comes. With the new pastor there is also an entry year, a time for learning about one another and beginning to build a healthy future together. In a calling denomination, we may have an additional interim year, as we seek to call a new pastor. Hence, we are dealing with three years and finding the wisest way to invest them.

I encourage congregations to see that sometimes it makes better sense to keep their current pastor and, constructively, use the same two-year period to focus on developing together. We frequently discover the next best church and the next best pastor in one another as we grow forward together.

## Moving and Staying

Across forty years of ministry, some pastors regularly move about every three or four years. They have ten new starts. A few pastors move every two or three years; in forty years of ministry, they have fifteen to twenty new starts. Every time a pastor has a new start, a congregation has a new start as well. Some congregations have had a new start with a new pastor every two or three years; they hardly get started before they start again.

Each year there is a high turnover of pastors among congregations. Much time and energy is invested in calling and appointing pastors. It was said of one minister that he had been in the ministry for twenty years. Someone wisely observed, "No, he has been in the ministry for four years. He has just done it in five different places." I encourage a goal of less-frequent turnover and longer, happy matches. We achieve this as we use the first three months well.

The art is to have an excellent new beginning in our early time together. The art is also to create a new start in a present congregation—whenever that makes sense. I affirm: we cannot make a first start a second time. We can make a new start, but a new start is not a first start. We get one first start together. After having been together some time, we can create a new start. It is simply this: the new start happens in the context of the first start.

On occasion, a pastor and congregation start off on the wrong foot together. It is not a bad start. It is not an excellent mismatch. There is the promise and possibility for an excellent match, but for whatever reasons the pastor and the congregation start off weakly—just as some people simply have an awkward and weak first date and yet go on to get married and live happy lives together. It is possible that a pastor and a congregation can recover from and move beyond a weak start. Basically, they do this by selecting a given three-month period and, together, following the suggestions shared in this book.

Most of all, I encourage pastors and congregations to have the fun of developing the foundations for a whole, healthy relationship in their early time together. Yes, we can recover from a weak first start, but why set up the need to do so? With modest planning and with good fun, we can create, in our early time together, an excellent beginning.

The art of a new beginning is to start strong and grow stronger. Begin well in your first start together. Leave the future open to God's leading. Starting strong means starting with the people and building strong, healthy relationships together.

Some pastors start weak. This leaves open the possibility that the relationship will grow weaker. The relationship may never develop richly and fully. The pastor and the congregation settle in to an awkward, unfulfilling relationship. On the other hand, with a new second start perhaps they can develop a healthy future.

A few pastors try to start in a loud, splashy way with all the things they plan to do to save or grow the church. It is a busy, noisy start, with much excitement, but it is at heart a weak start. They are bringing in their own agenda, not meshing with the congregation's agenda.

We begin with our new people, not with our own plan.

We begin mutually, sharing our wisdom and experience, our compassion and hope about life. We discover the richness of our relationships in ways of beginning. We learn with and from each other. We are grateful to God that we can share this life together with one another. With the grace of God, we grow forward an excellent match together.

The more people who share in the early time together, the stronger the beginning. The same is true for a new start together. We can encourage mission teams, grassroots groups, shepherding teams, worship teams, music groups, adult Sunday School classes, women's groups, men's groups, youth and children's groups, and committees to benefit from sharing in this new beginning time together. We head in the same direction for the coming three days, three weeks, three months, and three years. We are on common ground. We start strong and grow stronger.

# 3

# A Good Shepherd Visits

The grape pie was a surprise to everyone on the Welcome Team. As she set the dish down, Harriet, in her matter-of-fact way, simply said, "I have had more fun these past three months than I have had in years. I baked the pie to celebrate our good times together. Thanks for including me on the Welcome Team."

Janet brought a simple fruit dish of orange and grapefruit slices, served in that special bowl she discovered at some auction. Ben supplied the special coffee he dearly loved, made fresh for the gathering. Knowing Harriet and Janet preferred tea, he also brought several special herbal teas of which he was fond. Sue came with her familiar lemon pie, piled four inches high with thick, creamy meringue. Gene contributed a bounty of oatmeal cookies that tasted of honey and heaven. Truly, this was going to be a feast of desserts.

They had a great time celebrating together the three months that had so quickly come and gone, and gone so well. Indeed, the three months were better than they had anticipated. As the Welcome Team, they were pleased with how well their new pastor and the congregation were doing together.

The grape pie was the surprise.

Harriet was a legend for her grape pies. She loved making them. Her great-grandmother had originally developed the recipe, though people said that over the years Harriet greatly improved it. She took the grapes directly from her small vineyard out back. Joyously, almost as a sacrament, she mixed the ingredients. Her pie crusts were known for their delicate texture, richness, and crispness.

Years before, Harriet won best of the county fair for her pies. She won so regularly for a period of years that she finally decided not to enter anymore, to give others the fun of winning. She did continue to generously bake and share her special pies with friends in the community. She had great fun doing so.

Tall, thin, with rich, full gray hair, Harriet walks with a brisk, purposeful manner. Even in her seventies, her stride is long, and her path is straight. Frills and pretensions do not attract her. She does not gloss over things. Hers is a plain, matter-of-fact approach to life. She has the twin gifts of wisdom and generosity.

Five years previously, Dick had become ill. He was bedfast at home. He lingered long. She quit making her pies. She cared for him. They did not have family in the area. She became his primary support. She was glad to do so. They had had many happy times together.

Dick died two years before the feast of desserts.

People thought Harriet would return to making and sharing her pies. She did not. A year of quiet despair went by. Her grieving continued. She missed her husband. He had been her best friend. They had shared much of life together.

As the second year passed following Dick's death, Gene telephoned to ask her to serve on the Welcome Team. Harriet turned him down. She offered some flimsy excuse. She knew it sounded lame, even to her. Really, she was not up to it. Dick's death still lingered with her.

Three days later, Gene came by to visit with her. In his likeable, gentle way, he asked her again. She knew Gene did not have time to serve as leader of the Welcome Team. He had just become president of the company with which he had worked most of his life. His new responsibilities meant long hours, frequent meetings, and many new decisions. The grapevine said he was doing well. The company was beginning to prosper.

She was glad to see him. He was among the few people from the congregation who consistently visited and was helpful during Dick's long illness.

Gene's spirit peacefully fills a room. It is not that he is loud or boisterous. He is generally quiet. Many think of Gene as shy. To some extent, this is true. Mostly, it is his deep compassion with people and the gentle humility with which he lives life. He has a sense of joy and enthusiasm. His humor is subtle, good-natured. He helps people see the good in life.

In the midst of the conversation, Gene simply said, "Harriet, I need your wisdom and spirit on the team." There was a pause. The *no* almost escaped from her mouth. But reluctantly, she agreed to serve. Later, when she learned who else was on the team, she wished in passing that the *no* had struggled a little harder to escape from her mouth.

At the first gathering of the Welcome Team, she was glad that Gene was leading the discussion. She is a patient person. Nevertheless, she nearly said something she would later regret.

Ben can be infuriating with his quick opinions and pompous nature. Ben has the feeling no one listens to him, so he speaks loudly, interrupts frequently, and seeks to direct the meeting. It does not help that some years before this the personnel committee, in a moment of unwise desperation, asked him to serve temporarily as interim choir director while they searched for a new one. The one they had was excellent, but her husband's firm was promoting him to a new job in another state. Ben just stayed on.

But his directing the choir simply intensified his own pontifical behavior pattern. From that time forward, in any gathering, Ben began to behave even more pontifically, just as he would in rehearsing the choir. Some said it was because his father had been the same way until he died of his alcoholism. Others suggested that he learned the pattern from his stepfather, who joined the family when Ben was nine. Whatever the reasons, in a group Ben had a tendency to be as heavy-handed as he was heavyset.

His bass voice added richness to the choir. Most in the choir seemed almost satisfied with him as the choir director, but as they neared each Christmas and Easter, Ben would become more pontifical and domineering. His older sister said it was because the holidays were bad times for him; they were not happy times in his growing-up years. The memories of the family fighting, the shouting, the slamming of doors, leaving the house abruptly and angrily as his father and stepfather had done lingered long in Ben.

In day-to-day life, Ben could be fun, happy, flexible, and easygoing. He was always fixing something for someone in the congregation. He was especially helpful with the congregation's shut-ins. Martha still talked of his fixing her back door so it would keep the cold out in the winter. Mr. Treat was grateful for Ben's figuring out how to fix the low place in his kitchen floor, where he often stumbled and almost fell.

When Ben was fixing something, he was happy and cheerful. In conversations with one or two people, he would laugh and carry on, be pleasant, listen, and share. However, in a group of four, five, or more people, it was as if something clicked inside him and he sought to dominate the group. Fortunately, Ben deeply respected Gene, and Gene knew how to work with Ben.

Harriet was glad Sue was part of the team. Sue came to the community twenty-plus years before, taking over the history classes at the high school. Mrs. Pershing, beloved by all the graduating classes during the forty years she taught history, was retiring and moving to Florida. People wondered how Sue would do. The first few years were tough. No one in the town takes too quickly to a newcomer.

In her fourth year, people noticed that she went out of her way to help Billy. He was always a troublemaker in the community. She even helped Dorothy do well. Few thought Dorothy would ever graduate from high school, but she did and went on to flourish in college.

Slowly, the community discovered that Sue was an even more gifted teacher than Mrs. Pershing was. The parents and grandparents who had taken history under Mrs. Pershing discovered that their children and grandchildren came alive to school when they were in Sue's classes. She was accepted. She became an appreciated member of the community. Still, a newcomer. But now part of the family.

Harriet did not know Janet at all. She heard good things about Janet on the community grapevine and saw her at worship. They spoke briefly once or twice. However, it is hard to get around and visit with everyone before or after worship.

Janet moved to town during Dick's last year. She came to be the head teller at the bank. On the side, she did sewing for people. Even with her husband working as chief mechanic at the car dealership, it was tough making ends meet with three small children.

Janet's children sang in the church choirs. They were active on the community soccer teams. What impressed Harriet the most was seeing them frequently at the local library when she went to pick up and return the books that Sarah, her longtime friend and the librarian, secured for her through interlibrary loan.

The first gathering of the Welcome Team—Gene, Harriet, Ben, Sue, and Janet—was brief, to the point. Gene has a real gift for leading meetings like this. They agreed on the few areas of conversation on which they wanted to focus with their new minister and his wife, Marvin and Murlene. They would meet him next week, four weeks before he was to come. It would be a kind of advance orientation and getting to know one another.

Gene requested it. They had had good fortune in recent times with the ministers who came to serve their congregation. Nevertheless, the memory still lingered of the last two in a row, who did not match the congregation or the community. Those several years of disaster, offset by their happy memories of the many ministers who served well, led them to welcome a new minister with thoughtfulness and generosity.

The following week they gathered with their new minister. They were interested in Marvin sharing something of his life: where he was born, his parents and siblings, some of the events that happened to him in his growing-up years. Previously they had read the biographical material, and there had been a more formal meeting of the personnel committee with the denominational executive and with Marvin and Murlene.

They wanted this to be a personal conversation rather than a professional meeting. They were glad to share about themselves and were interested in Marvin as a person. The team wanted to know something of his interests and hobbies, his likes and dislikes, the things he enjoyed doing. They were interested in the kinds of people with which he had the most fun. They wanted to give him the chance to share something of himself and his family.

They made it a point to include Murlene, his wife, in the gathering. They were interested in her—her growing-up years, her interests, and the activities she enjoyed. They encouraged the two of them to share about their two sons. It was a conversation that, as both Marvin and Murlene later reflected more than once, pleasantly surprised them.

Always before, when they would go to a new congregation, the focus of the introductory meeting was primarily professional. There would be the polite, cursory talk of a personal nature at the beginning of the meeting. But the conversation would quickly shift to the history of the church, its current problems, and what the committee hoped they, as the new pastoral couple, would do to solve them.

This was new. These five people were interested in them. The minister and his wife realized later that the only conversation about the congregation itself was in discussing what the Welcome Team would do during their first three months to richly and fully welcome them into the congregation and the community. When Gene, on behalf of the team, outlined the possibilities with them, they were deeply appreciative of the thoughtfulness and generosity of the team. They looked forward to coming.

This would be new.

The Welcome Team made a basic decision. They wanted their new minister to begin with them—as persons. Thus, they began with him—as a person. They wanted their pastoral family to focus with them—as families. Thus, they began with them—as family. They wanted their new minister to begin with them as a good shepherd.

## Beginning as Family

People say to me, "Dr. Callahan, please help us find a pastor who will come and love us and whom we can come to love." Across the years, working with countless congregations, people again and again share these words with me in one form or another.

One congregation had difficulty getting a new pastor even

to consider coming to the church. One year, at my suggestion, they put on their application for a pastor these words, "We are looking for a pastor who will come and love us and whom we can come to love." A pastor became intrigued with the statement and went to visit. He fell in love with the people, and the people with him. He is their good shepherd and has been so for many years. The congregation is strong and healthy.

People have a longing for a pastor who genuinely cares with and for them. In a larger sense, people do long for, and look for, a good shepherd, a helpful preacher, a wise and caring leader, and a community pastor. The basic, beginning longing is for whole, healthy relationships of compassion between the pastor and the congregation.

One way I say it is this: the foundation of leading is love. People long for and look for a pastor who puts people first, who cares more about helping them with their lives than about the survival of an institution or the growth of an organization. People growth is more helpful than church growth.

A house does not make a home; people do. A building does not make a church; people do. A chart does not make a church; people do. Begin not with the plant or the policies, but with the people. The thirteenth chapter in I Corinthians does not end with the words, "Now abideth institution, organization, and church growth, and the greatest of these is church growth." The text is very clear: "Now abideth faith, hope, and love, and the greatest of these is love."

A congregation is a family. A large congregation is really a collection of smaller congregations, families, who have just enough in common to share the same leadership and pastoral team. In our time, and I think in most times, people long for a congregation, not an institution. They long for a family, not an organization. Begin with the family.

As pastor and congregation, with a healthy, mutual compassion, we learn and grow in this life. Together, we discover handles of wisdom and encouragement for living whole, healthy lives. We grow forward an excellent match as pastor and congregation so that together we can discover help, hope, and home in this life.

Thus, begin as a shepherd. In your early time, visit your regular worshipers, your shut-ins, and your people in hospitals.

When you are making a new beginning in a present congregation, do the same. Select a three-month period. With the help of a New Beginning Team, intentionally advance and deepen your shepherding relations with your regular worshipers, your shut-ins, and your people in hospitals. You can adapt what follows to the new beginning in your current congregation.

The focus of your visit is with the person you are visiting. There is a sacramental character to your visit. Your visit is an outer, visible sign of grace, compassion, community, and hope. Whether you are visiting with regular worshipers, shut-ins, or with people in hospitals, the focus is on the person you are visiting.

In one visit, with a given person, you can say, "Share with me about yourself." In a visit with another, you can say, "Share with me what you have fun doing." With yet another, you can say, "Share with me where you were born and what has happened since." Any of these possibilities are helpful beginning points.

These are invitations. These are not questions. There is no question mark at the end of the statement. Questions set up yes-or-no answers. They tend to be intrusive. With some people, questions have an accusatory sense. By contrast, you will be amazed what people share if you offer, with genuine interest and integrity, a simple invitation: "Share with me about yourself."

You learn as much by where they begin, as by what they share. They teach you, by where they start, what is primary with them, or what they think is important to you, or both. The person who begins with what he or she "does in the church" may be teaching you that this is central. Or the person may be teaching you that prior ministers have taught that this is what those ministers saw as important.

The person who begins with her family may be teaching you that her family life is central to her being. The person who begins with his work may be teaching you that his identity is in his vocation. The people who share of the volunteering they do in the community may be teaching you the love and mission they have discovered in their lives.

With many people, you may feel it is more natural to invite them to share what they have fun doing. I am amazed, as I share this invitation, how people come alive. They appreciate your interest in what they have fun doing. What we have fun doing is God's way of teaching us our strengths. Your simple invitation allows people to teach you their strengths.

The invitation "Share with me where you were born and what has happened since" is encouraging to many people. It is remarkable what people share. They give the highlights of their life. They share the people and events that have been important to them. They teach you of their hopes and their struggles, their good times and their tough times. Listen closely and they will teach you their fears and their hopes, their anxieties and their loves.

When you invite people to share their personal life stories, you learn of their history. In the process, you also learn something of the history of the congregation you now serve. They share about themselves, their family, their life, and how these have played out in the congregation.

However, if regrettably, you focus on asking them to tell you of the history of the church, three things happen. First, you learn the church's history. Second, you do not learn their personal history. Third, you teach them that your primary interest is in the church, not in them. It helps for you to focus on their personal history and life.

The primary intent of these early visits is fourfold: learning names, finding what you have in common, sharing strengths, and beginning a caring relationship.

## Names

Learn one another's names. Teach them your name as you learn their names. Concentrate on learning their names. The next time you see someone, call one another by name. It helps as you serve as minister and shepherd in their lives in the future.

Some lament that they cannot remember names well. This is a good time to unlearn that mistaken assumption. Our natural inclination—given to us by God—is to draw close to one another, to be in community with one another. It does take some energy to learn names. Sometimes, I think it takes more energy to work against one's natural gift of community and *not* learn names.

It is important that they discover and remember your name. Do not count on an announcement in the newsletter or bulletin to register in their minds. During the course of your visit, find ways to encourage them to remember your name.

One of the best ways is to focus on learning their names. Repeat their names a number of times during this first visit. This teaches them you have an interest in knowing them by name. The more interested you are in knowing their names, the more likely they are to be interested in learning your name.

## Finding What You Have in Common

Discover something you have in common. This can be at the deepest level of life's existence as possible. It may be a mutual interest or hobby. It may be friends, children, or family. The focus is on what you share mutually in daily life, not what you have in common in church life.

It may be where you grew up, or went to school, or visited on vacation. It may be some longing or yearning to help people with specific human hurts and hopes. It may be that you have shared together in some informal network of people. Perhaps you have common interests in certain community or recreational activities. Find some area of mutual interest, so that you can draw closer to one another as good friends.

## Sharing Strengths

Help people share their strengths, gifts, and competencies. Look for their strengths. Do not go looking for the problems. Look for what people do well. Once you find their strengths, then you have the foundation on which to build if you come to any problems. The art is to build on one's strengths.

Do not go looking for problems. They may come in due course. Look for what the person does well. A helpful way forward in ministering with people wrestling with alcoholism is to search for and discover the one strength, however fragile, feeble, and fleeting, that yet remains. On this rock, we build forward the future. If we focus solely on the problem, we become overwhelmed. We already are. The art is to help people share, discover, and claim their strengths. In so doing, they claim God's gifts.

## Beginning a Caring Relationship

Begin a sharing and caring relationship with one another. You are not trying to end a relationship. You are not seeking to accomplish in one early visit what appropriately develops over several visits. Sometimes we try to do too much in one visit. We want to be too helpful too soon. We allow our compulsion toward perfectionism to take over. We think this is the last visit as well as the first, and therefore we must do everything now.

Is there to be any visit beyond this first visit? Leave that open to the leading of God. For the moment, have a genuinely helpful first visit. Focus on the person and his life. Begin a shepherding relationship. The art is to quit while you are ahead. Leave before the person is ready for you to leave. Let this be, with integrity and simplicity, an excellent beginning visit. Leave well.

## Ways Forward

These four objectives—learning names, finding mutuality, sharing strengths, beginning relationships—make possible an excellent first visit. The focus is not on the institutional survival of the church. The focus is not on difficulties and dilemmas. Nor is the focus on a shortage of money. Whole healthy congregations never have enough money. They are always giving away more money than they have, and as a result God provides for them.

In your early time with your congregation, or in a new beginning in a present congregation, focus on visiting three groups. You can visit any of the following groups:

| | |
|---|---|
| Regular worshipers | Newcomers to the |
| Shut-ins | community |
| People in hospitals | People served in mission |
| First-time worshipers | Community persons |
| Occasional worshipers | Specific vocational |
| Key leaders | groupings |
| Recent new members | Specific geographical |
| Moderately active members | neighborhoods |
| Constituent families | Inactives |

In my book *Visiting in an Age of Mission* I offer a detailed discussion of each of these groups. The three most helpful groups on which to concentrate, in your early months, or in a new beginning in a current congregation, are your regular worshipers, shut-ins, and people in hospitals.

Someone may suggest you focus on inactives. Visiting inactives is like super pro ball. By contrast, visiting with regular worshipers, shut-ins, and people in hospitals is more like junior high and high school ball. These visits are comparatively straightforward. Certainly, in the long run it helps to visit with a number of the fifteen groups previously listed, depending on your community and the outreach of your mission. Early in a new pastorate, or while developing a fresh start in a present pastorate, it is central to visit regular worshipers, shut-ins, and people in the hospital.

There is power in visiting. People are helped. The gospel is shared. Lives are bettered, advanced, and made whole. We begin mutually helping one another in these first visits. You begin as a good shepherd.

# 4

# Possibilities for Visiting

The Welcome Team of Gene, Harriet, Ben, Sue, and Janet wanted to encourage a personal, family beginning with their new pastoral family. Together, they developed a thoughtful and generous three months of welcome with this focus. They decided, in consultation with their new pastor, to focus on regularly worshiping families, shut-ins, and people in the hospital.

Harriet asked Colleen, her long-time friend, to serve as leader of a team of people to arrange the congregational welcome after church on the first Sunday after Marvin and Murlene's arrival. Covered dishes filled the tables in the fellowship hall. There was a grand turnout. Many families came. Harriet, Colleen, and Gene stood with Marvin and Murlene in an informal, welcoming line just ahead of the tables holding the food. Everyone had the chance to meet the new minister and his wife.

Gene shared a simple, family welcome on behalf of the congregation in the worship service that morning. Over the meal, he did so again, more personally and informally. Everyone had a fun time. It was like a family reunion.

In the four weeks prior to their new minister coming, after the advanced gathering with Marvin and Murlene, Gene, Harriet, Sue, and Janet had arranged for the minister to visit with the regularly worshiping families in the congregation. These are families that worship, give or take, eight out of twelve Sundays.

There were about eighty such families. Actually, the team members' more specific goal was for the new minister to visit personally with at least one member of each of these families. Gene arranged visits with the twenty families he knew best. Harriet, Sue, and Janet did likewise. Ben agreed to help with the welcome in other ways.

In the advanced informal gathering, they had learned their new pastoral family was committed to a vacation trip the first two weeks of August and saving the remaining vacation for after Christmas, when they would journey to a family reunion to celebrate Marvin's parents' fiftieth wedding anniversary.

The team encouraged them to enjoy the fun of their planned vacation.

They would make the welcoming and visiting arrangements around those two weeks. The team also decided not to schedule anything for their new pastoral family the last few days of August. School would be starting up for their two sons. It would be a new school. Actually, it would be two new schools. Their older son was starting junior high. The younger would be in a new elementary school.

Ben had played right guard on the football team in high school, making all-state in both his junior and senior years. So naturally enough he said, "We want to start September with a rested quarterback, not a tired one." Marvin had not thought of himself in that way, but he did appreciate their consideration and thoughtfulness.

One reason they wanted to meet Marvin before his actual arrival was so they would have time to work out, in advance of his coming, this simple visiting schedule. They learned his way of working in that early conversation. They focused on the ten weeks that included the four weeks of July, the third and fourth weeks of August, and the four weeks of September. For each week, they arranged eight visits. They put together a visiting and shepherding schedule that matched his schedule.

Some of the visits were over lunch where people worked. Some were over morning coffee or afternoon coffee. Several were over breakfast. A few were at five o'clock. Virtually all of them were at or near where people worked. None were in the evening. Mostly, they wanted Marvin home with his family in the evenings, particularly in the early months.

They wanted their new pastor to come to know some of the regular worshipers early on. They wanted them to come to know him. They wanted to begin as family.

## Regular Worshipers

By starting with your regular worshipers, you immediately begin to develop shepherding relationships with the primary families in your congregation. You do something that perhaps no minister before you has done, and perhaps no minister after you will do. You gain the advantage of beginning with the lives of your people, not with the organization of an institution.

You begin in a personal way, not a planning way. You learn of your people's strengths and competencies, their hurts and hopes, their struggles and aspirations. You begin with your people, not with your plan.

You discover how your people have fun in life. The focus is on fun, not functions. To be sure, life brings its tough, difficult times. We have our share of sorrow and tragedies, sin and suffering. With the help of God, we find our way through such times.

We enjoy living. We are the Christmas people. We are the people of wonder and joy. We are the Easter people. We are the people of new life and hope. We are the people of the wedding feast, of the great banquet. We begin with who we are and whose we are.

We begin a relationship of trust and respect, integrity and credibility as we come to know the people whom we serve and shepherd. People begin to trust you as they know you like them and genuinely care for them.

## Visiting with Shut-Ins

While Gene, Harriet, Sue, and Janet developed the visits with the regularly worshiping families, Ben arranged similar visiting times with the congregation's twenty shut-ins. Over the years, Ben had developed close relationships with many of them. He was handy with tools. He knew how to fix things. His hands were flexible. For older persons, with hands gnarled by arthritis, this was a most appreciated gift.

Ben's younger sister occasionally commented that he liked doing things for "our older people" because they served, for him, as the parents he never felt he had really had while growing up. He was asked once why he spent so much time helping the congregation's shut-ins; Ben shrugged his shoulders, simply smiled, bashfully, gently, and said, "I don't know. I just like to. They make me feel good."

Ben worked it out for their new minister to visit with two shut-ins a week over the same ten weeks, beginning with those who were more seriously ill. He wanted their new minister to come to know them first. More important, because Ben arranged the visits, the shut-ins immediately received their new minister with the same warmth and affection they shared with Ben.

Your congregation may be in ministry with a wide range of shut-ins. There are those immediately related to your congregation as members, or in members' families. Some of the shut-ins your congregation may help are friends of your shut-ins, living next door, or sharing life in the same nursing home. Some may be community shut-ins, who have no congregation and no close ties directly to your congregation.

You will want to visit with all of them in due course. Focus first on the shut-ins whom your congregation considers as central to their life together as family. Several benefits and advantages result.

First, your shut-ins are helpful to you. They remind you of what you were called to do, namely, to be helpful in people's lives. In the busyness of institutions and organizations, we sometimes lose track of or forget what God invites us to do in ministry. We become preoccupied with the survival of a given local congregation. We become involved in denominational activities to help avoid the decline of the denomination. In our hurry and bustle, we sometimes forget to stop, look at one another, love one another, and be in ministry with one another.

Shut-ins share their wisdom. Their insights strengthen your perspective. You discover common sense on what is important in life. You find understanding on the distinction between needs and wants. You learn from them much of what is enduring in life—what lasts, what counts. They share their love with you.

Yes, one or two of your shut-ins may continue a pattern of complaining, lamenting, bemoaning, and whining that they learned early in life. This is not, primarily, because they are shut-ins. They were that way years ago. This is not primarily because of you. They are that way with most people. Mostly, your shut-ins share their love with you and help you know that you are cared for and well thought of. They encourage you.

Second, you are helpful with them. Your interest, your compassion, your good humor, and your caring prayers strengthen their lives. It is not so much that you are there to give advice or counsel. It is not that you are there to help solve major problems in their lives.

It is more that you are there to listen. The art of listening has almost been lost in this culture. We are so busy doing, acting, and talking that we have hardly learned to listen. Now, I do not mean that you go there for three or four hours, sitting like a well-worn bump on a log, wishing you were somewhere else.

I simply mean that for the brief time you are there, you are *really* there—listening, richly and fully. Yes, there is conversation. You enter in, mutually, sharing your wisdom and experience. Together, you share a helpful visit. They are glad you came. You are glad you visited.

Third, it is easier to have a funeral with a friend than with a stranger. Some of your first funerals will be with your shut-ins. Once you have visited with them and they with you, you can share well in the service for the funeral. The people in the service know you have shepherded the person who is now deceased. This is a comfort to them.

By contrast, if you do not come to know them well, you may struggle in the service. The service is formal and impersonal. There is a sense that you are not really part of the family in the service. People may be grateful you are present, but there is a sense of distance.

If you have visited with them, have some sense of their life pilgrimage, then at the funeral you speak from your own experience. Your sermon is more directly helpful. Your own grief helps those who are grieving. Your own understanding, however brief, of the person now deceased focuses what you share. The service is warm and personal. Family and friends are helped.

The fourth reason is decisive. People look for a pastor who helps them with their lives, even if there is no payoff, no gain, and no result of success for the pastor, the organization, or the institution. Sadly, a few pastors have focused just enough on payoff, on what's in it for them, or what's in it for the growth of the church. This causes people to ask, perhaps not aloud, but quietly and sincerely, "Does this pastor do what he does based on serving people, or on gain for himself and the institution he represents?"

The few pastors who focus on gain may not do so consciously. Nevertheless, they allow themselves to be almost instinctively drawn to the big givers, the persons who fill their committees, the ones who flatter their egos, and the ones who make their church grow bigger. There are not too many pastors like this. Regrettably, there are just enough. Thus, people—young couples, the middle-aged, senior adults, and youths—wonder whether we now have a pastor who will be helpful in our lives when there is no payoff.

Unfortunately, in recent times there has developed a preoccupation about whether congregations are growing bigger. Some people, caught up in fixation on church growth, have even said that visiting with people is no longer effective. What they really mean is that since the goal is church growth, visiting is no longer effective because it does not immediately increase the size of the church.

Visiting *is* effective in people's lives. It may or may not be effective in increasing the size of the church. But growing bigger is not the primary goal of the church. Again and again, people share with me the value of a visit from a pastor whose compassion and caring, whose wisdom and encouragement help them with their lives.

God must think visiting is effective. The text says, "And

God visited and redeemed His people." The text does not say, "And God stayed in heaven and redeemed His people." Our God visits us and redeems us. Our God invites us to do as God does, namely, to visit with people.

In the life of Jesus, it is clear that he spends considerable time visiting with people—on hillsides, in homes, at the sea, and in marketplaces. He visits with the well and the troubled, the poor and the rich, the healthy and the sick, the dying and the dead, the sinful and the struggling. The early disciples spent enormous amounts of time visiting with people. Paul's visits with people across the Roman empire were legend.

A visit is a gift of grace. It is a sacramental sign of grace, compassion, community, and hope. There are no strings. There is no payoff anticipated. It is not a manipulative means to some bigger growth. In the end, people sense that some pastors do what they do as a means to some end. People discover, with appreciation and gratitude, that many pastors do what they do to serve their people.

This is clear in visits with shut-ins. There is no payoff. Shut-ins are not going to increase worship attendance. They are not going to join committees. They are not going to go on this or that work project or fill some empty slot as a Sunday school teacher. They are not going to sing in the choir and increase its numbers. They are not going to call on first-time worshipers and newcomers to the community. They are not going to increase membership. Their giving may be modest.

With integrity, faithfulness, and distinction, shut-ins do their best work as shut-ins. To be a shut-in is to have a place of honor and dignity, to be worthwhile, to be a person, to be a source of compassion, humor, and wisdom—and to be a focus of your compassion. Many shut-ins carry on a ministry of wisdom and encouragement through telephone conversations, personal notes, and letters. In recent times, some shut-ins are doing so though e-mail and the Internet.

In the parable of the Samaritan, the question comes, "Who is the good neighbor?" I frequently think the good neighbor is the man in the ditch, robbed and beaten. Who is the good neighbor? The good neighbor is the one who draws forth the best in others. The good neighbor is the man in the ditch who drew forth the best in the Samaritan—the man who in centuries come and gone has been called the Good Samaritan.

In visiting that is mutual, it is never quite clear who is helping whom. Sometimes, the person we think we are helping is really helping us live our lives at our best—to live a life of grace and compassion. We visit shut-ins not because we feel sorry for them. We visit them because they are God's people. We are here to be helpful in people's lives even if there is no payoff. We do the mission for the sake of the mission.

When you visit the shut-ins of your congregation, you teach all the people of your congregation that you plan to be helpful with them in their lives—even if there is no payoff. We do the mission for the integrity of the mission, not for payoff or success.

My grandmother died when she was about ninety-seven years of age. She was a person of joy and wonder. She knew how to live life, to have fun, to laugh, to play. Some of us are still learning how to do that. She was a great source of wisdom and joy, fun and laughter.

She spent the last ten years of her life in a nursing home— not the best, not the worst. In her latter years, she spent much of that time in bed. Our family visited. Friends visited. In addition, across the years she lived in the nursing home, the two groups who regularly visited her were from her Sunday school class and from the Salvation Army.

We think well of her church. We think well of the Salvation Army. They visited with a person when there was no payoff. They did it with integrity and for the sake of the mission.

These days, much of what I do to help with the Salvation Army I do in honor of and appreciation for those visits they shared with my grandmother. Through the years, as they were sharing those visits, they were not in any way aware that I was her grandson. They visited her with a sense of mercy and compassion, caring and hope.

Their visits stirred my interest in helping them. Thus, I have taught for a number of years at their School for Officer's Training in Atlanta. I have spoken to a wide range of Salvation Army gatherings, served as retreat leader in officer's councils, and as consultant to a range of Salvation Army projects. I have lost track of the local Salvation Army Corps, Boys and Girls Clubs, rehabilitation centers, and camps I have had the privilege of visiting and helping.

Get to know your shut-ins well. You will help them. They will help you begin your ministry at your best.

## Visiting in Hospitals

I have already shared with you, in Chapter One, the decisive impact of Tom's visit in the hospital that Friday morning. You will remember that, on Thursday, Tom and his family moved into their new home. They were coming to serve a difficult, troubled congregation with a record of many losing seasons.

The denominational leader encouraged Tom to know that not much was expected of him. Pastors had come and gone, been battered and bruised, and done their fair share of battering and bruising as well. Tom was being invited to serve this congregation simply to "do the best you can."

Tom did two things. One, he went to a hospital on a Friday. Two, he shared his willingness to visit with people in the congregation. For those two acts, within three days of being there, in the years come and gone, Tom is the legendary shepherding pastor of that congregation.

The less shepherding, the more bickering. The more shepherding, the less bickering. Sometimes, a congregation experiences years without the help of a shepherding pastor. More often than not, the congregation ends up in a pattern of bickering and complaining, whining and lamenting. To be sure, in such a congregation it may help to focus on conflict resolution or organizational advances. What helps, most frequently, is the sharing and caring of a good shepherd.

As you visit in the hospitals, you become a good shepherd in the lives of many people. Your visits are particularly helpful with people and families facing difficult illnesses. I encourage you, in your hospital visiting, to feel free to visit people who are part of families in your congregation, even though they are not be members of your church. Also, feel free to visit with people in the hospital who are friends of members of your church. Your visits are especially meaningful if these people have no church home of their own.

Your visits in hospitals need not be long. They are visits of grace and hope. They are not preoccupied with church stuff. These are gentle visits. The focus is with the person and her life. You share compassion and good spirits. You have prayer with some of the people you visit. You may feel it appropriate not to do so with others. Your presence is a prayer in their lives.

In your visits to hospitals—especially during your early weeks—visit with the nurses, the doctors, and the staff of the hospital. They benefit from your shepherding as a caring pastor as well. They are helpful to you. Together, you can become a team for healing and heath.

Janet is widely respected at the hospital. She is a volunteer in the hospital auxiliary. Equally important, perhaps more so, the bank for which she is the head teller is the one the hospital uses. Thus she has many business dealings with the hospital and its employees in a given week. The hospital trusts and appreciates her, remarkably so.

Thus, in one of the early weeks of his being there, one gift she gave to Marvin as her new minister was that she took him to the hospital. She took him around and introduced him to many of the nurses, doctors, and staff. A further gift was that in doing so she lent to Marvin her own considerable credibility and integrity.

## Visiting Possibilities

You and your Welcome Team will discover, among several possibilities, the simplest ways to accomplish these shepherding visits. I encourage you to use this guiding suggestion: visit with people in the same way they visit with each other in daily life. In our time, people visit over lunch, breakfast, morning coffee, afternoon coffee, and after work. People visit with each other less in the evening at home.

People live where they work. People sleep at their houses. This is my shorthand way of saying that people in our time frequently live in what I call their "vocational village." It is most natural and easiest to visit your regular worshipers where they work. You will have fun over lunch with one or several of your regular worshipers who have the custom of lunch together. They will be happy to have you join them.

With some people, you can have the fun of morning or afternoon coffee where they work. Not with everyone, but with some. Some people catch breakfast near where they work. Feel free—on a Thursday—to have breakfast together, where they work or near where they work. Some in your congregation may be in the habit of stopping for coffee after work on their way home.

These are five opportunities to visit: lunch, morning coffee, afternoon coffee, breakfast, and after work. Over the course of a week, this gives you twenty-five possibilities. One of the difficulties in visiting is finding enough evenings to visit. Here are an array of possibilities.

Your Welcome Team has the gifts and graces to schedule these visits for you. They can set a time that works for both of you. They can organize these visits before your arriving at the church. You spend your first days visiting, not organizing the visits.

You have the triple benefits of visiting your regular worshipers, getting to know the people at their work, and coming to know the community more fully. People teach me they are both amazed and grateful that a pastor came to their place of work. It is likely no pastor has been there before, and likely that no pastor will ever be there again, save for your shepherding visit.

I still remember Tony's minister. I put my way through school digging ditches, running a ninety-pound jackhammer, and finally working up to being a form setter for highways and roads. Tony was foreman of our construction crew. We were sitting on the edge of the ditch, having our thirty-minute lunch break. Tony's minister walked up, sat down on the edge of the ditch with us, and visited with us as we ate. He had a sacramental presence about him. He shared his good humor and his compassion. He was interested in us.

In the New Testament, we discover Jesus calling His disciples when they were at work, fishing. Yes, Jesus visited people in their houses as well. Some of the richest pictures of Jesus are with the people on the hillsides, at the seashore, and in the marketplaces where they work.

It is not possible, for various reasons, to visit some people easily at or near where they work. That is fine. Your Welcome Team can decide, in consultation with you, to arrange a visit through a small-group gathering, or a visit in your study, or a visit in their home.

Frequently, someone in the congregation is happy to sponsor a small-group get-together in their home or in a community gathering place. In this small group, you have an opportunity to begin to know some of your people and they to know you. This gathering is informal, good fun, a good time, and the focus is on the people who come.

You can have fun visiting with some people in your study. Some people, in their own work, call on others at their offices. They will be happy to come and visit with you in your study. Some people prefer to visit this way. Your Welcome Team can schedule a time that works for both of you.

With some people, you will want to share this early visit with them in their home. You can do this on a one-family, one-house basis. This is especially true of your shut-ins who are living at home. Alternatively, in some cases, you can visit with two or three families who are close friends, in one of their homes. Orville and Mary and another couple, Harold and Wilma, frequently gathered at one another's home of an evening to visit together. Two or three families may have a habit of gathering at one home in the normal course of their lives together.

The natural way forward is to visit with these families in the way they visit with one another. Later, you can visit each house. In these early days, you are seeking to come to know the persons who are your regular worshipers.

You and your Welcome Team will think of other ways forward. Some constructive combination of one or more of these possibilities helps.

## A Simple Plan

With your team, develop a simple plan so that you begin, or begin anew, as a good shepherd. For example, a congregation with an average worship of 150 is about 200 to 250 persons.

It takes more people than 150 to achieve an average worship attendance of 150. Some come every week, some two or three times a month, some once a month. There are those who come now and then, and those who come on Christmas and Easter.

Two hundred and fifty people represent between ninety to one hundred households. Of one hundred households, sixty to eighty are likely to include regular worshipers. That is, they worship eight out of twelve Sundays. Focus on ten of thirteen weeks. Your visiting plan for the ten weeks might look something like this:

| *Type of Visit* | *Households* |
| --- | --- |
| Work | Forty |
| Small groups, two with ten households in each | Twenty |
| Study visits | Eight |
| Home | Twelve |
| Total visits | Eighty |

Visiting plans vary based on the customs in the community.

Because of the nature of the congregation and the community, Gene and his Welcome Team decided to focus on a combination of work visits and home visits. They created a simple plan for ten out of thirteen weeks—eight visits a week with regular worshipers, mostly at work, and two visits with shut-ins in their homes.

Gene and the team knew it was not possible, in the early weeks, to visit with everyone. Indeed, a pastor who tries to visit everyone in the early time ends up visiting no one. When we set too many goals too high, to be accomplished too soon, we postpone action to postpone failure. Procrastination is not the problem. Compulsion toward perfectionism is the problem.

Progress is more helpful than perfectionism. It is not possible in the first few weeks to do everything. The effort to try to do everything ends up being the decision to do nothing. In consultation with Marvin, Gene and the team decided to do a few things well.

To some, this sounded like a very leisurely pace. Janet said, "We want a leisurely, purposeful pace. We want our new minister *present* in these visits, not simply there with his mind elsewhere. Further, we are leaving room for what may come up. We want our new minister to begin as a good shepherd."

## Wisdom and Compassion

I encourage you to be wise and caring in these shepherding visits with regular worshipers, shut-ins, and those who are in the hospital. Repeatedly, as I ask congregations about pastors they remember best and cherish most, they talk of the pastors who came to love them, and whom they came to love. Some congregations look back twenty years to the shepherding pastor who lived with and loved them best.

You are here to love the people God has given you. You are here to love the people in the way in which God loves you. Be wise and caring in your love. Your people will not always be lovable. You and I are not always lovable.

You have not come to push and shove, organize and administrate, boss and dictate. You are not here to whine and complain, challenge and commit. Your task is not to manage and manipulate. You are not here to share your pet peeves and passive aggressions. You are not here to displace your depression and despondency. You are not here to prophesy and predict, persecute and point.

When you marry into a family, you marry the whole clan. You get Uncle George, with his marvelous sense of humor, and you get Cousin Rupert, with his dour countenance and dire depression. You get Aunt Mabel, with her wisdom, and you get Brother John, with his foolishness. As best you can, you learn to love the whole clan. Remember, they also get you with your own idiosyncrasies and peculiar ways.

Do not be naïve in your love. Do not pretend that all people are wonderful and joyous. Some have a compulsion toward perfectionism. Some have a passive sense of power-lessness. Some have an excessive drive toward achievement. Some have deep depression and dependency. Some look for codependent-dependent relationships. Some are angry. Some lie, cheat, and steal. Some do awful things under the cloak of respectability.

We are all sinners and stand in need of the forgiving love of God.

When we are naïve in our love, we become cynical in our actions. For pastors who are cynical (and for that matter, for everyone who develops low-grade cynicism in their lives), the real problem is not cynicism. The real problem is that they have been naïve and thereby disappointed. As a result, they have developed cynicism. A naïve view of love is the devil's way of trying to develop cynicism in us.

Develop a constructive, healthy love with your people that is mutual and wholesome. The real shepherds are not the ones who love their people in cozy, syrupy, sentimental ways, nor in warm, fuzzy, foolish ways. Be wise and caring in your love. Share understanding and forgiveness. Share peace and hope. Together, you are more fully open to the grace of God.

A visit is a gift of God, freely given, with no strings at-tached. I have always thought of a visit as a "warm call." When I have lunch or morning break, knock on a door or visit with a small group, I think of my best friends. I am both grateful and amazed at how many new best friends I have lunch with, or who open doors to me, or whom I discover in small-group gatherings.

In your early time, do this well: visit with your regular worshipers, shut-ins, and hospital patients. God blesses your early weeks together. It is fun to be the legend on the community grapevine for loving your people. You share good shepherding not to become the legend but because of your genuine interest in people, in their lives and destinies. The happy by-product is that in your early weeks you become the legendary shepherd in this congregation, in this community.

Gene, Harriet, Ben, Sue, and Janet had a wonderful feast of desserts. Ben's special coffee and tea were excellent. Sue's lemon meringue pie was among her finest. Janet's fruit dish of orange and grapefruit slices was a welcome inclusion. Gene's oatmeal cookies were delicious. Harriet's grape pie was the best of all. Harriet had come home. They laughed and carried on. They had done solid work. Their new pastor was on his way to becoming a good shepherd.

Give yourself the gift of beginning as a good shepherd. Give your congregation and community the gift of beginning as a good shepherd. Together, richly, fully, you will discover grace, compassion, community, and hope.

# 5

# Visiting Your Way to Helpful Preaching

I opened the door, hesitantly, reluctantly. It was Sunday afternoon, around two-thirty. We were not expecting company.

We had moved into the house on Shadydale a few days before. We were renting it. The house was around thirty years old, with gray, worn shingles on the outside. There were two small bedrooms, a bath, a living room, and a small dining area off a still smaller kitchen.

We moved there to be nearer the university, and to be closer to a grade school for our two sons. There was a yard for them to play in. We hoped there were children with whom they could find friends. We had been living in an apartment complex some distance away, but the commute was more than we anticipated.

We came to this strange, vast city, not knowing anyone. We still had many boxes to unpack. The house was cluttered. The first night we discovered the colonies of roaches that lived there. There seemed to be a different colony for each room in the house. It had stood empty for some time. In showing us the house, the owner mentioned in passing that the house had recently been "treated."

Where we came from, the problem was termites; and so we breathed a sigh of relief that we would not have to deal with termites. However, in the area of the country to which we were now moving the problem was roaches, not termites. He did not have the house "treated" well enough. We did battle from that first night. We were winning, but our progress was slow.

We went to a nearby church that Sunday morning to worship. It was our first time. We stopped at a cafeteria for a brief lunch. We came home, changed into work clothes, and now, on that Sunday afternoon, we were continuing our unpacking. We hoped to bring some sense of order to our new home.

I opened the door.

Bob Taylor was standing there, with his warm smile and gentle manner. He had one foot on the first step to the small front porch, and one on the ground. His tall, lanky frame bent slightly forward. His graying hair gave a quiet dignity to his pleasant, somewhat aging face.

He had come to visit with us. He was senior minister of the large, regional church in which we had worshiped that morning. He thanked us for worshiping with the congregation and for filling out the visitor card. He wanted to welcome us to the church and the community.

We invited him in, and made room, amid the mess, for him to sit down. I do not remember what he said, or what we talked about in his short visit. I do remember three remarkable things. He came. He was interested in us. He shared with us a spirit of genuine compassion.

We knew we had found home.

For the many years we lived in that city, we were active in that church, attending worship and participating in a wide range of programs. Our sons, as they grew older, were active in the youth program. Julie and I contributed much volunteer time with the program. I coached the church basketball teams. We helped with a number of church projects. We found friends and family with the congregation.

All this began with the gracious, shepherding visit of Bob Taylor.

The next Sunday, when we went to church, we felt his preaching was even better. We have treasured his influence in our lives for many years.

## Shepherding and Preaching

The more shepherding, the better the preaching. There is a direct correlation between shepherding and preaching. A pastor's preaching, on a scale of 1 to 10, is a 7. The pastor is a good shepherd, and so the preaching is heard as a nine. By contrast, for a pastor whose preaching on a scale of 1 to 10 is also a 7 but who is a not a good shepherd, the preaching is heard as a 5. It is a lot more fun to be heard as a 9 than a 5.

The foundation of listening is love. People listen to the person who loves them. By beginning your visiting with your regular families, you immediately advance your preaching. They hear you better. As they discover you have a genuine interest in them as persons, they listen more fully. They hear you less well if they think your interest in them is primarily to get them to be committee members, bigger givers, or Sunday school teachers. People care in the same way they are cared for.

People listen in the same way they are listened to. In our shepherding, as we listen, three quietly remarkable things happen. First, we learn, more fully, the art of listening. Second, we teach people the art of listening. Third, because we listen, we learn. We learn more when we are listening than when we are talking. The person who listens is listened to. The person who does not listen is not listened to.

This dynamic is equally true when you are seeking to develop a new start in a current pastorate. In our own families, we sometimes become so busy with this activity and that project that we fail to share, even with our own loved ones, our interest and compassion with them. The same is true in churches. We become busy with this project or that program, this policy or that plan. We lose sight of people. Our intentional visits deepen our shepherding relationships with our people.

The sooner you visit your regular worshipers, the more at ease you feel in your preaching. This is especially true in a new pastorate. When you look out on a given Sunday and you know many of the people who are there, you are at your most relaxed. You have a sense of presence and peace, confidence and assurance. You have a warm feeling of being at home with family.

The more quickly you come to know your people, the sooner you relax.

When you look out on a group of strangers, the sermon is more distant and awkward, the halting pauses more present, the "uhs" more frequent. You feel removed and separated from the congregation. When you look out on a group of friends and family, you can be your most relaxed. Each Sunday as you look out on your congregation, you see familiar faces. It is a lot more fun to preach with a group of friends than it is with a group of strangers.

When most of the people are strangers, we become tense and tight, nervous and anxious. Our compulsion toward perfectionism stirs. We tend to deliver cluttered, crowded sermons. We try to do too much, to be too helpful. Our sermons contain too many suggestions, set too high, to be accomplished too soon. We overwhelm people with more than they can absorb or do.

If the pastor becomes tense and tight, this tends to cause the congregation to become tense and tight. The early months of preaching are less well done. If the pastor is relaxed and having fun, the congregation does likewise. If we are having fun, we are more likely to move forward. Under tenseness, people wither. With fun and encouragement, people grow and develop.

The sooner you come to know your people, the more helpful your sermons are. Your preaching is more focused. As you quickly get to know your regular worshipers, what you share in the service and the sermon, the music and the message is more immediately helpful in their lives. Most pastors want to be helpful in people's lives and destinies. Shepherding is clearly the simplest, easiest way to begin accomplishing this goal early in your ministry.

Further, the sooner you feel at home with your regular worshipers, the more welcoming you are with first-time worshipers and occasional worshipers. If you are clearly at home, you help them feel more at home as well. Your sense of quiet confidence and genuine compassion helps them know they have found home.

First-time worshipers teach us that they are searching for a sense of home. They bring with them a search for community, not committee. The more relaxed and genuinely at home you feel, the sooner they feel at home. Likewise, occasional worshipers teach us that if they have a church home at all, it is here. Otherwise, they would be occasional worshipers somewhere else! Their presence is not accidental. Even though they may not be present every Sunday, they have some sense that this congregation is home. The more at home you are, the more at home they are.

One of the strongest, healthiest congregations in this country was built by a pastor whose sermons, on a scale of 1 to 10, were—Sunday after Sunday—a 4 or 5. Were you and I to attend a first time, we would hear him mumble and mutter a sermon, with hardly any outline or sense of direction to it. Yet he is a legendary shepherd in the community. He is ever-present in people's lives. He is better known in the hospitals than the doctors are. He has baptized, married, and buried more people than anyone in the community. When someone who does not have a church needs help with her life, she calls him. Sunday after Sunday, people hear his sermons as a 10. These are the words of their good shepherd.

## Your First Sermon

On your first Sunday, begin a preaching relationship with your congregation. I use the word *begin*. Have the confidence of knowing that your first sermon is a beginning point. If there is any mistake people make in their first sermon, it is that they try to accomplish too much too soon. They try to hit a home run. Feel free to hit a single.

This is the first inning of the game, the first chapter of a book, the first block in a quilt, the first verse of a song, the first step in a journey together. We are not trying to preach a sermon that covers everything for the next three to five years. We are beginning a pilgrimage together as God's people. Let the first sermon begin, not try to end, the journey. Let the first sermon lead us in a given direction.

This is equally true if, as a minister, you are starting anew with a present congregation. Let the spirit of your sermon, at the beginning of this three-month period, lead us in a new direction, with the fun of beginning a new chapter in our life together as God's people.

Your first sermon is *not* on the state of the church. I encourage you to stay away from a sermon on the future of the church. Your people have already heard enough of those to last them several lifetimes. Many of your predecessors have provided a rich, full bounty of such sermons. As I interview people, some teach me they know these sermons almost by heart.

The fundamental problem with a state-of-the-church sermon is that it has an institutional, organizational focus. Regrettably, you immediately teach your people that your primary interest is in the church, not in them—that in a sense, you see yourself as having come to oversee a church rather than shepherd a congregation. Such a functional focus does not help as a beginning point.

You may find it useful to give such a sermon once you have been there six to nine months. You will sense when such a sermon is appropriate. Certainly, it is fitting after you have developed (or, in the case of a new beginning with a present congregation, deepened) significant shepherding relationships with your people. Then your sermon more naturally focuses on the future of the congregation. It focuses on your life and mission together as a congregation. This is a person-centered, people-centered, relational sermon rather than a functional, institutional, state-of-the-church sermon.

In your first sermon, teach your people you are interested in them and in their daily lives. You can share a sermon that helps with a specific human hurt and hope. You can deliver insight and resources that help with a significant stage of life. Your sermon may have something to do with how we experience new beginnings in life. We do experience a wide range of new beginnings through the course of this life's pilgrimage: the new beginnings of first grade, high school, a marriage, a new job, a new home.

We experience new beginnings as we grow and develop whole, healthy lives in the grace of God. In this life, we do have our fair share of anxiety and fear, anger and rage. We do experience worries and concerns, griefs and disappointments, celebrations and good times. We most profoundly experience hope-filled events. Through these events, we know that God's grace encourages us, Christ's compassion surrounds us, and the healing hope of the Holy Spirit leads us forward.

Let the focus of your first sermon have to do with life. Your people will leave with the sense that the sermon directly helps them advance and build their lives.

Your first sermon need not be weak and timid on the one hand or harsh and demanding on the other. These are the two extremes. The first is hesitant and halting, superficial and slick. It skims the surface of life, without really helping. The second is severe and querulous; the sermon comes off as fussy and imperious, with a latent acrimonious shadow. It communicates law, not grace. Although frequently delivered with a mild-mannered, soft-spoken voice, such a sermon nonetheless has an underlying message of law.

Let your first sermon share your best, current preaching on grace. Let the sermon have about it a sense of confidence and assurance. In theme and manner, communicate a spirit of compassion and a sense of community. Share your wisdom and your encouragement. Know that your sense of presence and manner is as important as the theme of what you say. Who you are helps people hear what you say. People look forward to your coming sermons as a result of your first sermon.

Sometimes a sermon has two endings, or three. The minister does not quite know how or when to end. It is like someone who visits in your home and sits on the couch like a bump on a log, hardly speaking, while you carry most of the conversation yourself. Finally you begin to wonder if he plans to spend the night, whether or not the guest bedroom is made up, and if you have what he might like for breakfast.

At a given point, a sermon has a diminishing return. This is particularly true in the first sermon. The first sermon is the first step in our journey together. The first sermon is not the first ten miles in your journey together with your congregation. You are beginning—with confidence and assurance, compassion and community, encouragement and hope—the first *step*.

Start strong and grow stronger. Begin well in your first sermon and grow forward your preaching in the weeks to come. I would suggest that the first sermon be helpful and *brief*. The problem many have with the first sermon is trying to do too much too soon. In your first sermon, as well as in most of your preaching, quit while you are ahead. Quit before people are ready for you to quit. They will look forward to the coming Sunday.

## Your Strengths for Preaching

Mark and I were discussing his move to a new congregation. We were sharing our morning break in a restaurant near where he worked. He wanted to visit with me about preaching. He was deeply troubled as to whether his preaching would measure up to what was expected of him. The pastor before him had been a solid preacher. His predecessor's sermons were genuinely helpful in people's lives, and his delivery was excellent. Mark said to me, "He will be a hard act to follow." With a kind of sad sigh and worried forlornness, he went on to say that he did not see preaching as his "long suit."

I encouraged him to be himself in his preaching. "It's a mistake for you to try to be like your predecessor. You cannot be him. You can be you." I shared two suggestions with Mark.

First, he should focus on the major Sundays in the coming three months. And second, he should develop his sermons on the strengths *he* brings to his preaching. I encouraged him to avoid any temptation to do his preaching in a manner that was not his own.

With respect to my first suggestion, I encouraged Mark to focus his preaching on

- The first Sunday
- The two major Sundays across the three months
- The last Sunday in the three months

My experience is that pastors who focus on these four Sundays across a three-month period do well in their preaching. Pastors who try to be up for every Sunday, thirteen sermons in a row, do poorly. I encouraged Mark to have the fun of sharing his most helpful preaching on these four Sundays.

We discussed the first Sunday earlier in this chapter. As for the two major Sundays across the three months, every congregation has certain Sundays that are special to them. The possibilities include Pentecost, Sunday of the weekend at the Fourth of July, vacation Bible school Sunday, August picnic on the grounds, rally day, homecoming, Christmas, Easter, Mother's Day, and many more. The major Sundays vary from one congregation to the next.

The art is to look at the three months ahead. Discover the two major Sundays. Focus some of your best sermon preparation on these two. Do so even before you launch the three months. Look to these two Sundays as high points in your preaching, high points in the sense of being richly helpful with your people. They will remember these two sermons. On these two Sundays, the message and the music, the sermon and the service are among the most helpful in their lives.

With the last Sunday in the three months, have a similar spirit as with the first Sunday. This is not the occasion to deliver a state-of-the-church message. Rather, it is simply one of the four Sundays across a thirteen-Sunday period in which your preaching is most helpful with your people. If you do so, people will look forward to the coming three months.

Most people do not expect a pastor to be up in his or her preaching every Sunday. Oh, a few people may, but they are like that about everyone and everything in their lives. The vast majority of people in a congregation are wise enough to know that they are not up every day in their own jobs, let alone in their own lives. They do look forward to the few good times that give their lives a lift and help them move forward.

Mark began to relax as we discussed the four major Sundays in his three early months. He could see these four as possible.

With respect to my second suggestion—to develop his sermons on the strengths *he* brings to his preaching—we looked at his specific strengths for preaching. I took a paper napkin from the holder on the table. On it, I outlined the possibilities with which pastors grow their preaching and touch the lives of their people. (I discuss this in depth in *Preaching Grace*.) For the purposes of my conversation with Mark, I outlined the eight possibilities on the napkin:

| | |
|---|---|
| Presence | Motivation |
| Preparation | Delivery |
| Resources | Structure |
| Content | Outcome |

We focused on which of these he does well. He concluded that his lead strengths are preparation, content, and structure.

We discussed which *one* of these current strengths he could expand and which *one* new strength he could add. He confirmed he was seeking to develop his strength in content. He wanted to add motivation as a new strength in his preaching. We talked of how he could grow forward these two strengths.

I encouraged Mark to focus on these strengths in his early preaching. The pastor before him, as best we could discern, had preaching strengths in presence, content, delivery, structure, and outcome. His predecessor was especially known for his excellent delivery. Mark was becoming too preoccupied with his own delivery. At the present, this was not what he did best. Indeed, to him it was a considerable weakness. The more he focused on delivery, the tenser and tighter he became about his preaching. I suggested to him that, in due course, he could grow forward his delivery. For now, he could best continue on the course of growth he had already set for himself: content and motivation.

Confident content leads to confident delivery. To some extent, I overstate the point to make the point. Content without delivery helps people. Delivery without content is so much fluff. Confident content has a spillover effect of advancing confident delivery. The preacher who believes his or her message delivers it better. The passion for the message advances the poise of the delivery.

To this end, I invited Mark to share with me several of the Scriptures that mean the most to him in his life. I encouraged him to explore, in fresh, new ways, the meaning of these texts for his own life and the lives of his people. This would lead him to new discoveries that help him and his people in their common life's journey together.

He would be sharing helpful insights into everyday, ordinary life in the light of the gospel. His preaching would have a spirit of confidence and assurance precisely because he would be preaching out of his strongest convictions and understanding about life. Both his themes and manner would communicate compassion and community

I said to Mark, "The content of your preaching will be rich and full when you base it on the texts and convictions that you find helpful to you in living this life." Now, I do not encourage pastors to announce a twelve–Sunday series of sermons entitled "My Most Helpful Convictions" or "My Strongest Convictions." Further, I do not have in mind your strongest convictions in the sense of challenge and commitment. There is more at stake in the early weeks than simply challenging your people to deepen their commitment so that "we will have a better future together."

In the three months, particularly on the four major Sundays, share the Scriptures that mean the most to you in your own life, in your own journey. Share the insights, the discoveries that help you live a whole, healthy life. Share the wisdom you have discovered that helps your sense of individuality—of integrity, autonomy, identity, and power.

Share the foundational convictions that help you in your search for community—for roots, place, belonging, family, and friends. Share the insights that help you discover new meaning—purpose, value, and significance in everyday, ordinary life in the light of the grace of God. Share the resources of hope that help you live with confidence and assurance—trusting in hope in the present, the immediate future, the distant future, and the next life.

I encourage you to use the lectionary in the early weeks and discover the texts designated for each Sunday. As you do so, I invite you to think through which of these lectionary texts have been, and are currently, most helpful to you. However, in the early months I do not encourage you to follow the lectionary rigidly, slavishly, as through it were law.

The lectionary is grace. The lectionary is guide. The lectionary is resource. More than anything, it helps you and your people in your early weeks if you share the texts, insights, and convictions that are helpful and strong in your life. "In this way," I said to Mark, "you will advance both the content of your preaching and the lives of your people."

We then discussed the area of motivation. This was the one possibility that Mark wanted to add as a new strength in his preaching. I outlined for him the five major motivations that draw people to the church, that help them be workers and leaders and give generously of their strengths, time, and money. These major motivations are compassion, community, challenge, reasonability, and commitment.

In chart form, I outlined them on another paper napkin:

|  | Key Leaders | Grassroots Members | Pastor, Staff | Unchurched |
|---|---|---|---|---|
| Compassion |  | X |  | X |
| Community |  | X |  | X |
| Challenge | X |  | X |  |
| Reasonability |  |  |  |  |
| Commitment | X |  | X |  |

Frequently, the two major motivations among key leaders are challenge and commitment. To be sure, the other three are present, but the primary ones are these two. Thus, key leaders teach a new pastor that what they need in their church is people who rise to the challenge and deepen their commitment: "We need more commitment. Then, things will be better."

For a new pastor, this appeal by key leaders triggers sermons that focus on challenge and commitment. At the end of the service, the key leaders positively reinforce such sermons. They say, "You really gave it to them today." "Be sure to hit them harder next Sunday." "Keep up the good work." The key leaders and the pastor are on the same motivational wavelength. In early meetings with one another, the key leaders and the new pastor focus on challenge and commitment.

The difficulty is this: the grassroots folks and the unchurched motivate themselves with compassion and community. It is as though the pastor and key leaders are broadcasting on the wavelength of challenge and commitment, but the grassroots people and the unchurched have their radios tuned to compassion and community. The emphasis on challenge and commitment comes across as so much static.

It creates a motivational gap. Further, what it does among grassroots members is grow passive-aggressive behavior, low-grade hostility, subliminal resentment, and eruptive forms of anger. It does not motivate people at the grassroots level and it does not reach the unchurched.

I drew a second chart for Mark:

| | Key Leaders | Grassroots Members | Pastor, Staff | Unchurched |
|---|---|---|---|---|
| Compassion | X | X | X | X |
| Community | X | X | X | X |
| Challenge | | | | |
| Reasonability | | | | |
| Commitment | | | | |

"This is a motivational match," I said to Mark. "The earlier chart is a motivational gap. If challenge and commitment were going to reach the grass roots, these motivations would have done so by now. They have surely been worked hard enough by the key leaders and your predecessors. It is not accidental that they have not worked. The grassroots people do not respond to them."

I suggested that, at the appropriate time, he draw the two charts for some of his key leaders, showing them what both a motivational match and a motivational gap look like. Further, I encouraged him to help his key leaders rediscover what drew them to this congregation in their own earlier years. They would talk mostly about the sense of love and compassion they discovered in the congregation. They would speak of the spirit of community and home, of roots, place, and belonging, that they found with this group of people.

But, in the years come and gone, weighed down by the institutional baggage of trying to keep the "bloomin' venture afloat," they have left less well-tended the very motivations that drew them to the congregation. They have nurtured forward the motivations of challenge, reasonability, and commitment.

When someone says to me, "Dr. Callahan, what we need in this church is people with more challenge and commitment," I say to them, "What you have taught me, good friend, is that you are a longtime Christian." (A primary reason so many of the books on discipleship speak of it as commitment is simply because they are written by longtime Christians.) The early motivations that draw all of us to the Christian movement are compassion and community. Years pass. Some of us grow forward the motivations of challenge and commitment, and some do not.

I usually go on to say, "If there were lots of longtime Christians out there, we could do well on challenge, reasonability, and commitment. What is out there are people new to the Christian movement. What is out there are grassroots people who are drawn to compassion and community."

I invited Mark to share with me how he had found his own way to the Christian movement and to the ministry. He spoke of the sense of compassion, of love and acceptance, that he found in his home congregation. He described the spirit of family and community he discovered with this group of people.

I shared with Mark my own experience. I described growing up in First Church, Cuyahoga Falls, Ohio, and of the sense of roots, place, and belonging that I discovered with the congregation. I found home there. The first pastor I ever knew well was George Whiteman, with his stocky build, slow-moving walk, and gentle smile. He was a shepherd. I shared with him my memories of George McClausland, who served as the associate minister, of his good humor and caring spirit. He called the square dances in the social hall, visited the sick, and loved the people.

I spoke of Paul Acker, who served as the senior minister when George Whiteman moved on. Paul Acker's preaching stirred my soul. He encouraged my longings to the ministry. He advanced my understanding of the grace of God. I do not remember what he said, nor do I remember what he preached. What I remember is his compassion with me. What I remember is his love of the congregation and his passion to be their shepherd. What I remember are his gestures of kindness. His genuine love with and for me helped shape the course of my life.

I said to Mark, "People care what the minister knows when they know the minister cares. The foundation of learning is love. The foundation of leading is love. The team plays well for the coach who loves the team."

I encouraged Mark not to make the mistake a few ministers do. Namely, during the week they are good shepherds with their people and share compassion and community. Regrettably, on Sunday morning, in dull, deadly boring sermons, they hammer on challenge, reasonability, and commitment. Their people say, "Pastor, you do not seem quite like yourself when you are preaching." Their people have excellent insight.

In the closing of the Gospel of John, Jesus says, "Peter, do you love me?" Peter responds, "Yes, Lord, you know I love you." Jesus says, "Peter, feed my sheep." The text does not say, "Peter, will you rise to the challenge? Peter, will you make the commitment?" Jesus knows Peter is an early Christian, not a longtime one. Thus, the focus of Jesus' invitation is on compassion and community.

Mark and I had an excellent conversation that day. We reflected on the people who, whether from his past or now in the present, mean the most to him in his own pilgrimage. We discussed the influence they had and continue to have in his own growth and development. We discussed the motivations with which they related to him. I encouraged Mark to grow the area of motivation in his preaching by relating to his congregation in the same spirit of compassion and community with which his mentors have related to him.

By expanding his current strength in content, and by adding a new strength in motivation, Mark would have the sense that he is growing his preaching. His focus on these two would have a spillover impact on some of the other strengths. He would preach with a sense of confidence and assurance, knowing that his preaching is advancing and that his sermons are touching the lives of his people.

## Helpful Preaching

As you prepare your early sermons, ask yourself (particularly on the four major Sundays), *How does this sermon help people with their lives and destinies in the light of the gospel? How does this sermon help people discover the grace of God?*

In our time, people long for and look for helpful preaching. In earlier times, people may have looked for great preaching. However, what people teach me, in interviews and small-group conversations, is how our preaching is helpful in their lives. They are not looking so much for alliteration, sophistication, the turn of phrase, or polished prose. What they look for is something that helps them live their lives during the coming weeks.

People are looking for a helpful sermon, not a great sermon. It is not that your sermon on a given Sunday needs to be the sermon to end all sermons. It does not need to go down in history as the most remarkable sermon ever. You are putting too much pressure on yourself when you think that way, particularly in this new beginning time. People long for a sermon that helps them. They are not interested in whether the sermon is destined to be published or printed in some journal or book, or whether the alliteration and structure of the sermon have the poetry of a masterpiece. They long for a sermon that helps them live life.

When you share a helpful sermon, four remarkable, decisive events happen:

1. Your people are helped.
2. Your people come to know you as helpful.
3. You stir their confidence and assurance.
4. They make new discoveries in their lives.

In a helpful sermon, you share your wisdom and experience, your new discoveries and insights about life. You share your hopes. You discover the richness of the Scriptures, with fresh, new insights about life now, in the present. You help your people get to know you and your insights and discoveries in ways that help them with their lives. As you share your best wisdom early on, you help your people with their own search for individuality, meaning, community, and hope.

As you are sharing your wisdom and experience, insight and discoveries, you are at your most relaxed. You have a sense of peace and presence. You preach with confidence and assurance. Most important, you are helpful as you lead your people to discover resources for a whole, healthy life in the grace of God. People experience help in their own life's pilgrimage. They say, "Ah, now we have a pastor whose preaching helps us with our lives."

Bob Taylor never came back. He did not need to. He had helped our lives. His visit that Sunday afternoon was decisive. The shepherd and the preacher were one. He was our pastor from that Sunday on. We became part of his congregation because he became part of our lives. Our time in that vast city was richer and fuller because of him. He lived what he preached. He preached what he lived. We were together with him many times across the years. We learned from his caring. We learned from his preaching.

In your early months, I encourage you to let your shepherding and your preaching enrich one another. An important part of sermon preparation is shepherding. Let your first sermon begin both a shepherding and a preaching relationship with your people. In these weeks of new beginning, let the focus be with their lives and destinies. Build your preaching on your strengths for living a whole, healthy life. Grow your sermons with the specific strengths you bring to preaching. Focus on helpful preaching, especially on your major Sundays.

Live grace. Share grace. Preach grace. God will bless your preaching.

# 6

# Leadership Starts Now

I was helping one congregation. Willard and I were visiting, my first day there, in the afternoon. The sunlight was streaming through the windows. One of those remarkably beautiful days we cherish in life. Willard is one of the central leaders in that church. He and his carpentry team had built the original sanctuary, now used as their chapel. Next, he and his construction company built the Christian education building. More important, he and his firm then built the new sanctuary, one of the finest in the region.

The congregation is part of a denomination that historically did not allow women to vote on congregational matters. Many years ago, at the national level of that denomination, the policy was adopted that women could vote—potentially—and it was left to each individual congregation to decide the matter for itself.

Willard said to me, "Dr. Callahan, I see our congregation as an island in the lake." Translation: all the other churches in the denomination in that community had individually decided that women could vote on congregational matters. Willard's church had not. In his view, his congregation was upholding the historic tradition of the past.

I said, "Willard, either the island is sinking, or the water is rising, and you and I had better build a bridge to the mainland, or find us a boat, before we are the last ones left on this island as it sinks." We talked long that afternoon.

Josh came as pastor six years before. He favored women voting. He was considered a liberal. In the late spring, after he had been there a year, he called a congregational meeting to decide whether women could vote. Willard gathered people out of the woodwork to defeat the proposal. They won by several votes.

The next year, and for five consecutive years, Josh called for a vote, and five times Willard gathered people to defeat the proposal. Their liturgical year became: Christmas, Easter, The Vote. The most recent vote was two weeks before my arrival. There was still a lot of heat left.

The second day there, Josh and I were headed to a meeting in his car. I said to Josh, "I have a puzzle. You were here as pastor six months when your secretary said it would be helpful to her if the bulletin could be done on Thursday rather than on Friday. Your response was, 'I have always done the bulletin on Friday, and I don't plan to change now.' A couple of years passed from that comment. She asked once again about the possibility of the bulletin being done on Thursday rather than Friday. Your response, more firmly and rigidly, was, 'I have always done the bulletin on Friday, and I don't plan to change now.'

"Recently, she and the personnel committee together requested the possibility of the bulletin being done on Thursday rather than Friday. Your entrenched response was, 'I have always done the bulletin on Friday, and I don't plan to change now.' You shared much of this with me yesterday.

"Josh, I have this puzzle. On something as simple as the bulletin being done on Thursday or Friday, your response is, 'I have always done the bulletin on Friday, and I don't plan to change now.'

"On something major, foundational to the historic identity of this congregation, your message is, 'Please change now.' Help me understand this puzzle."

There was a long, long silence. We rode two whole blocks. We sat at a long traffic light. Finally, Josh said, "I see what you mean."

I said, "Josh, I have another puzzle. You teach me, your congregation teaches me, that your best preaching happens on Sunday night. You study the text. You consult the commentaries. You pray for your message. With a simple outline, you share a warm, insightful sermon. Your people leave with what I call handles of help and hope.

"On Sunday morning, you virtually read a long, tedious manuscript sermon. Both you and your people teach me your preaching on Sunday evening is most helpful. I advise you, from now on, to make Sunday morning Sunday evening. Each Sunday morning, share the best Sunday evening sermon you can. If then, on Sunday evening, you read a manuscript sermon, it won't do that much damage and harm."

That day, I suggested to Josh that he make these two changes in himself, simply and quietly. I suggested to him that people would sense his own flexibility and growth. I encouraged him not to set up a bargain—namely, his saying he would make these two changes if women would be allowed to vote. Bargaining would not help. What helps, what gives his people confidence and assurance that they can change, is that they sense his own willingness to change, to be flexible.

Some time passed. As I remember, ten to twelve weeks came and went since I shared my two suggestions with Josh. Willard called me long distance, just before we were to leave for Australia. He said, "Dr. Callahan, would it really work for women to vote in our congregation?"

I said, "Yes, Willard, it will work, and you will be remembered years hence as the person who built the original sanctuary, now the chapel, the education building, and the new sanctuary. Most especially, fifty years from now, you will be remembered as the person who built the bridge to the mainland."

Then, I said, "Willard, you will want to deal with the ghost of your mother in some other way." Ghost of mother. You always ask yourself, when someone expends as much energy as Willard had over five years, gathering people out of the woodwork, *What is going on here that is not apparent?*

The reason we talked long and late that first afternoon is because we were talking about his growing-up years. He was the oldest of four. He was seven years old when his father deserted the family. His mother took her anger, bitterness, and resentment out on her oldest son.

From the time he was seven until he became fifteen, she beat him up, emotionally, physically, spiritually. When he got to be fifteen he was big enough to beat her up. But rather than do that, he ran away from home, got a job as a carpenter's helper, and worked himself up, over the years, to running his own major building firm.

I said, "Willard, you will want to deal with the ghost of your mother in some other way. It is not fair to her. It is not fair to you. It is not fair to the congregation you dearly love."

Three things happen in that congregation today. One, the bulletin is done on Thursday. Two, every Sunday morning, Josh preaches the best Sunday evening sermon in the area. Three, women vote.

## Grow Forward Some Things Now

This phrase is my way of saying: achieve some advances now. Make some changes now, both in yourself and in your congregation. Regrettably, some people say, "Make no changes in your first year." That really sounds like: "Make no advances and no improvements in your first year."

There is no point in making a change just for the sake of change. Some things are simply matters of personal preference. Feel free to honor lots of the personal preferences your congregation has. You do not need to impose your personal preferences upon them. If you do, they will simply respond by seeking to impose their personal preferences on you.

Whether the name tags are yellow or blue at a church supper on Wednesday night is a personal preference. Whether the choir wears robes in the summer or not is a personal preference, the practice of which varies widely from one congregation to the next. Whether the tables in the fellowship hall are set up running east to west or north to south is a personal preference, not worth being concerned about in your first three months, if ever. Be at peace about lots of personal preferences.

At the same time, know that one of your best chances to make *some* advances and improvements happens in your first three days, first three weeks, first three months, first six months, first year. Some suggest it is easier to achieve whatever advances you are going to accomplish in your first three to twelve months, and that they are more difficult to bring about later. My experience is that in about half the congregations where I have served as consultant, it is clear that the best chance for some improvements happens in the first three to six months. In the other half of congregations, the best chance for advances happens in the third, fourth, fifth, sixth, and seventh years.

## Personal Advances

In helping Josh and Willard's congregation I discovered what I now call the two for one principle: make two changes in yourself for each one change you hope for in others. Another way I share this principle is: be flexible in yourself in two ways for each one way you hope your congregation will be flexible. Ask of yourself what you ask of others. For each point of flexibility you hope for in your congregation, be flexible yourself in two ways.

A new beginning is an excellent time to decide to grow yourself. They do not know you. They do not know how you have always done some things in the past and, therefore, they cannot anticipate that this is how you do them now. You can leave behind some old habits. You can put in place some new habits. You can grow and develop. People count on, hope for your development. Your growth gives them encouragement. It provides an example of how they can develop themselves. People sense a growing person, and your growth gives them confidence and assurance.

When you decide to make a new start in your present congregation, do the same. Select two personal changes you plan to grow in yourself. Now, you do not need to tell your congregation, whether new or current, the specific old habits you are leaving behind. Nor do you need to share with them the new habits you are putting in place. Nor do you need to do this by bargaining. Do not say, in effect, that you will make these two changes if they make this one. This does not help. Simply grow yourself. Without your saying anything, they sense that you are growing and developing in your life and your ministry.

Fortunately, an increasing number of pastors see these early months as an excellent time to make changes in themselves that they hope to make. Pastors who are making a new start with a present congregation do the same. They see these three months as a new opportunity to grow themselves in their life and their ministry.

Think about the injunction that says, "Make no changes in your first year." Regrettably, that is precisely what some pastors do. They make *no* changes. The difficulty is that they make no changes in themselves during the first year either. They hear the first three words of the injunction: "Make no changes," and that is what they do. They wait. They mark time until the first year passes.

Increasingly, pastors are intentional about coming to know their people. They do not wait for it to happen, almost accidentally, by osmosis, across that first year. They are aware that underneath the old adage of no changes in the first year is the principle "Get to know your people well before making too many changes."

You can do much toward getting to know your people in your early months, especially as you benefit from the suggestions in this book. You can intentionally achieve in three months what some ministers take a year or more to do. The basic suggestion is this: the sooner you come to know your people, and they come to know you, the sooner wise and knowledgeable advances can happen. Because you know one another, the changes happen with a spirit of mutual trust, respect, and integrity.

Simply and quietly, make the two changes that help you grow you. People gain confidence and assurance that they can change as they see your creativity and growth. Grow forward yourself in two ways for each one way you hope other people will grow forward. People take heart from your example.

The spirit of flexibility includes flexibility in oneself, not simply counting on flexibility in others. As pastor, Josh counted on flexibility in his congregation. With our conversation that day, he discovered flexibility in himself. We learn a spirit of flexibility, a willingness to explore and experiment. Sometimes, regrettably, we are tempted to learn a spirit of rigidity and sameness.

When we become inflexible with ourselves, we tend to become inflexible with others. Our spirit of inflexibility contributes to other people's becoming inflexible. The more inflexible we are, the more inflexible they become. We share and receive rigidity and inflexibility. We develop an unhealthy working relationship. Life becomes complex. Fortunately, the more we grow, the more likely others are to grow.

We cherish change and flexibility in others. The key is our own personal range of growth and flexibility. You can teach yourself to grow. You can create a new range of flexibility in yourself. As you do so, you become wiser and more thoughtful in the flexibility you ask of others. Think of simple changes you can advance in yourself. Think of new ways you can practice a spirit of flexibility. As you do so, you become, even more so, a wise, caring leader with your congregation.

One way to think about it is this: if you cannot change anyone else in your congregation, at least change yourself. You control you. No one prevents you from growing you— except you. You grow you. Nobody else can grow you. If you discover you are leading a reluctant, planning-to-make-no-changes congregation, focus first on your own growth. Make healthy changes in yourself.

Leaders first lead themselves. Leadership begins at home, with you. One who has learned how to lead oneself is in the best position to lead others. Leadership is guiding on a way. Being a leader is first learning how to lead and guide oneself on the way.

Leaders have some sense of where they are headed. It is the principle "I cannot control what others do. I can control what I do in relation to others." The best way to be a leader is first to lead oneself, and then lead others. I am invited to lead many seminars on leadership. Most often, the underlying message of the invitation is, "would you come and teach us how to lead others?" In the early stages of the seminar, the first thing I do is help people discover how to lead themselves.

I am impressed, again and again, with the many people who participate in the AA and Al-Anon movements. They make substantial changes in their behavior. They are living their twelve-step plan, one day at a time. They are growing and developing whole, healthy lives. My spirit is: if they can change and grow, so can we. Decide on two changes you plan to make in yourself. Decide your plan for personal improvement, before you decide your plan for congregational improvement.

## Congregational Improvements

As you make two changes in yourself, in your new beginning, it helps to make one change in your congregation. The key in congregational improvements is to focus on a 20 percenter. This is especially true in this new beginning time.

Concentrate on the "20–80" principle: 20 percent of the things a person or a group does delivers 80 percent of the results, accomplishments, and achievements. One way of understanding the principle is this: two out of ten plays win football games. The art, what takes wisdom, is discerning which two plays will win the game. Save the 80 percenters that only deliver 20 percent of the results for a later time.

The 20–80 principle does not mean 20 percent of the people do 80 percent of the work. It does not mean that 20 percent of the people give 80 percent of the money. I am in churches where 10 percent of the people are doing 90 percent of the work. I am in churches where 30 percent of the people are giving 70 percent of the money. Wherever you see a few people doing most of the work and a few people giving most of the money, what you find is not the 20–80 principle. What you find is a *motivational gap*.

As we discussed in the preceding chapter, a motivational gap is created when the key leaders—motivated by challenge and commitment—broadcast on the wavelength of challenge and commitment in an effort to mobilize the grassroots members. The catch is that the members mobilize themselves on another wavelength, with the motivations of compassion and community. A broadcast sent out on the wavelength of challenge and commitment comes across as so much static.

There is no resonance. There is no match. There is no communication. Grassroots listeners, tuned to the wavelengths of compassion and community, do not hear the appeal to challenge and commitment. Thus, the same few people end up doing most of the work and giving most of the money year after year. The grassroots people help actively and give generously—when they are invited to do so with a spirit of compassion and a sense of community. If the focus is on challenge and commitment, key leaders respond to those motivational resources; the grassroots members do not. The art of your new beginning is to discover at least one 20 percenter that delivers 80 percent of the results. Share this key priority with your congregation with a sense of compassion and a spirit of community.

Sometimes, in their enthusiasm, a new pastor and congregation go off on a planning retreat. They fill three walls with newsprint of all the things they can think of, think about, possibly almost consider the thought of maybe doing in the coming three years. With much eagerness, they turn all the newsprint into a thick, ninety-seven page, long-range planning document. It does two things well. One, it sits on a shelf that would otherwise be empty. Two, it gathers dust that we would otherwise have to gather in some other part of the galaxies.

The best long-range plans are one to two pages, five pages at most. What takes wisdom is to discern, of all the things we *could* do, which are the few key 20 percenters that *will* deliver 80 percent of the results for our future.

# Foundational Reasons

In this new beginning, I encourage you to make two significant changes in yourself and one 20 percenter in your congregation. It is fairly easy to see the foundational reasons for the two improvements you make in yourself. Clearly, the two changes you make in yourself will benefit you. You will be a healthier person. The two changes benefit your family and the people around you. You are easier to live with. You have more fun and are more fun. The practice of your ministry is richer and fuller, more helpful with your people.

I want you to understand the reasons for making one key change in your congregation. This is not to be an incidental change. Nor is it accidental. It is intentional, wisely done, and with a spirit of compassion. I encourage you, early on, to discover, and make at least one 20 percenter change in your congregation. There are three reasons.

## The Congregation Expects It

If you do not make any key change during a whole year and then try to make some change, they will be surprised, caught off guard. After all, you have lived with the way things are for a whole year. "You did not do anything about it," they say, "while we were expecting you to do so. Why are you making these changes now?"

They may or may not like the change you decide to make now. Some people may express their feelings that they want you to leave things as they have been. Nevertheless, they are wise enough to know that a new pastor brings new ways of shepherding, preaching, and leading.

Try not to make too many changes in your early months. You can overdo it. Your presence is, in itself, a change. Thus, if you go on to make five to ten major changes on top of that, you are overloading people's capacity to deal with change.

They will resist the changes. What is more damaging, they begin to resist you.

Simply, gently, make one helpful change. Look for an "easy" 20 percenter. Select a change that leads people to action, that mobilizes their best energies and creativity, that moves them beyond sitting and waiting. Choose a change that is an advance, a genuine improvement. Do not make a change merely for the sake of changing.

Try to choose a change that is not merely a matter of your own personal preference. One pastor had a preference for serving communion by intinction. Without consulting with anyone, the first Sunday he served communion in that manner. The congregation resented and resisted. They were off to a weak start together. On top of that, he quickly changed many things in the bulletin, the order of worship, and the newsletter. He reorganized this and restructured that. It was too much too soon.

When he and I visited, I asked him why he chose to serve communion that way. Specifically, it was the one change that most offended the congregation. He said, "I like doing communion that way. It is for me a matter of personal preference." It was not, for him, a matter of theology. He simply preferred doing communion that way.

We discussed whether he had the habit of doing always what he liked to do, or whether, in daily life, he honored other people's personal preferences as well. I asked him whether he honored some of his wife's personal preferences, or whether he insisted on his own ways. We discussed whether he honored some of the preferences of his children and his close friends. He did. "Then," I suggested, "you can do the same with your new congregation."

Try not to make foolish changes. A few pastors seem to learn a propensity for how to start a fight. They pick something to change without thinking it through. They fail to visit with key leaders and grassroots people. They do not invite the wisdom and experience of other people. They do not lay the groundwork for the change. They simply make the change and then wonder why they find themselves in turmoil with their people.

When a change is made with wisdom, compassion, and consultation, people tend to respect it. They know you have done your homework. It is not a flippant, impulsive change. You have thought it through. You have talked it through. The key is to select one 20 percenter change that, long-term, advances the strength and health of your congregation.

## You Are Leading
You will want to assert your leadership constructively and significantly in your new beginning. If you do not, you lose some of the early power that is vested in any new leader. A new pastor begins with a certain range of power, goodwill, and influence. The art is not to squander it in too many directions, nor invest it in foolish changes that are ultimately inconsequential. Similarly, do not wait too long to discover a key improvement and assert your leadership. If you wait too long, you teach people that you do not know how to be a wise, caring leader.

When you assert your leadership in one constructive direction, people respect you as a leader. They learn to trust your wisdom and judgment, your vision and common sense. If you wait too long to do so, not only are people surprised, but in addition you are doing so at the tail end of the early goodwill and power they vest in you. It is too late. You have spent too much time teaching them you are not a leader. On the other hand, if you assert your leadership early on with integrity and fairness, you teach your people that you have come to be, with them, a leader.

If the change works, be graceful. Be easy to live with. With integrity, be gracious, be grateful. Be neither haughty nor prideful. Should the change not work out, should you "lose," do so with integrity. Do not pout. Do not become depressed. Do not take it personally. You may simply have selected the wrong change to implement. Even then, you have asserted your leadership, and what is finally important is that you teach both yourself and your congregation that you are a wise, caring leader.

## You Are Helping

There is likely one change, one advance that in fact helps. It is likely to be a highly visible quick win. With some congregations, we are sufficiently on the brink of the abyss that unless some advances happen soon we are over the brink and at the bottom of the abyss. Most congregations are not in that precarious plight, but many benefit from some one change that advances their strengths and health now.

Some congregations have been slowly weakening for years. It is a gradual, almost indiscernible decline. They continue downhill in their old patterns of behavior. They almost know that those ways no longer work. They sense that, if something does not change, they will continue to decline. They may resist the change—but many of us resist change at the outset. The art is to select a key advance that genuinely improves the health of the congregation.

Try to avoid chasing rabbits. It is amazing to me how quickly we allow ourselves to get sidetracked into chasing rabbits. Do not allow yourself to become embroiled in these pursuits. All families have their share of minor conflicts. Likewise, most congregations have their share of minor conflicts. As best you can, stay clear of as many of them as possible. If one crosses your horizon, immediately *refer* it to one or two people who can make a wise, thoughtful decision.

In a family, a minor conflict may have something to do with whether the toothpaste tube is squeezed in the middle, or neatly rolled from the end. In a congregation, it may have something to do with where the kitchen utensils are supposed to be kept. Somebody may have moved them from where they have always been.

Someone presents you with this minor disagreement, or that petty conflict. This fuss has been going on for years. These fusses are continual sources of conflict for the people involved and ongoing amusement for the people who watch. As best you can, do not allow yourself to be drawn into chasing these rabbits. Stay on the main trail. Have some sense of where you are heading.

What counts in your first few weeks and first few months is to discern a few 20 percenters. Wise, caring leaders focus on the 20 percenters. They have the confidence and assurance, the wisdom and discernment to know that these few 20 percenters deliver 80 percent of the results. A positive example of a 20 percenter is your shepherding with regular worshipers, shut-ins, and those in hospitals. Another 20 percenter is doing some of your most helpful preaching within the first three months. Organizing yourself is a positive 20 percenter.

You will find several other 20 percenters that advance the future of the mission in your community. Sharing a one-time event that helps children and their families through offering fresh, new resources for their lives together is a 20 percenter. Developing a remarkable one-time event that is helpful with the youth of your community is a decisive 20 percenter.

Among the several you find, select one to implement now. The art is to focus on what is important, not what is urgent. Wise, caring leaders have the capacity to distinguish between needs and wants. The needs are the 20 percenters that help people become a whole, healthy congregation richly and fully. The wants are the things we might want—this gadget, that trinket, something else—but they are not central to serving God's mission.

Discern what is foundational, what is fundamental. Have the wisdom to look for the key improvements that are "people wins," not "paper wins," that advance people in their lives and destinies. They focus on person-centered objectives that encourage the strengths, gifts, and competencies of the congregation. When you focus on what advances the health of the congregation, people discern that you are not changing things just for the sake of changing things. You are building and growing forward. You are advancing and improving the health of the congregation in the grace of God.

## Save for Later

In your new beginning, save several activities for later. One of these is *organizing your books*. "Nest" with your congregation, not your books. Organize yourself, not your office. Save unpacking your boxes of books until later. What profits a man if his books are organized, but he does not find his congregation? What profits a man if his library is organized, but he is not?

There was a time when, in the first few days after a move to a new congregation, I felt compelled to organize my library of books. My books are like children. They are part of the family. I know them by name. We have lived together well, and I have learned much from them. I have lots of books; it is a large family. I know precisely where each of them belongs, on which shelf, beside which books. I felt I had to get the family organized in my library, before I could really do anything.

Feel free to organize the *few* books that are your key books. They may be your Old and New Testament books and commentaries. They may be a few books on church history, theology, and mission. They may be your books that have to do with shepherding, preaching, and leadership. Have this core set of books well organized in your early time. Indeed, you can intentionally pack this basic set of books before you move. In unpacking, it is easy to put them in place. Then, leave most of your other books in boxes. Save organizing those for a later time. Yes, it is impressive to have all those books on the shelves. When your people come into your office, they discover how learned and well read you are.

I realized, one time as I was unpacking and organizing my family of books, that I was nesting in my new place. We all want to nest in some way. It dawned on me that it would be more helpful to nest with my people. If I could only get one project organized, it would be more important for me to come to know my people, early on. I already knew my books. I decided it was more important that I nest with my people.

What genuinely impresses your people is your love with and for them. What really stirs them is your compassionate shepherding and your helpful preaching. Your people count more than your books. Except for a few essential books, leave the rest in their boxes during your early time.

A second project to save for later is *developing a newsletter*. Some congregations benefit from a newsletter. If the congregation has a newsletter, let it continue in its own grace and peace. Do not spend time trying to improve it. If your congregation does not have a newsletter, feel free not to start one during your first three months.

I am very much interested in communication. In most congregations, the grapevine is the most powerful form of communication there is. A newsletter is further down the list. Moreover, regrettably, newsletters tend to focus on institutional and organizational matters, such as committee meetings, programs, activities, and budgets.

The best communication that can happen in your new beginning is on the community grapevine. People talk of you as a shepherding pastor who has come to love them as they come to love you. When they talk of your preaching, their comments are of how your sermons are helping them to live whole, healthy lives. Save the concept of a newsletter for later.

A third item you can save for later is *improving the bulletin*. If your church does not have a bulletin, do not start one during the first three months. Many congregations worship God without having a bulletin. This is particularly true in congregations where the majority of people in the congregation have not yet learned to read. Indeed, across this planet, there are many thousands of congregations where people can read; nonetheless, they gather each Sunday to discover the grace of God without a bulletin.

Should you discover your church has a bulletin, let it continue in whatever good ways it has with whichever people are doing it. Should you discover that the practice is for the minister to do the bulletin, you may—with grace and in good spirits—decide to continue that practice. You may discover two or three people who would have fun doing the bulletin but have just never been asked. You may also decide that during the first three months you will have a bulletin primarily on special occasions.

If it turns out that the bulletin is something the minister has customarily done, be at peace about it. Do it simply and graciously—with dignity and decorum, integrity and honor. However, do not spend a lot of time trying to improve and advance it, or moving it to a more complex stage of development. Do it simply. Save any improvements you want to make in the bulletin for a later time.

A fourth matter you can save for a later time is *being the church secretary*. Some congregations have a volunteer, or part-time, or full-time church secretary. Secretaries come with a range of strengths and gifts. The range of competencies falls into these categories: administrative coordinator, administrative assistant, executive secretary, general secretary, clerk typist, typist, and clerk. These are not titles. These identify the various competencies that secretaries have.

When you discover you have a volunteer, part-time, or full-time church secretary whose range of competencies is that of an administrative coordinator, administrative assistant, or executive secretary, know God has blessed you well. Encourage her, listen to her, learn from her, stay out of her way, and give her the chance to double your effectiveness. She knows what needs to be done next. She will help you even before you have thought of it, and she will have it done, please just sign. She knows how—quicker, faster, and better than you do—to deal with phone calls, appointments, meetings, calendars, and administrative projects. She is of immense value to you

On the other hand, you may find that the secretarial help available to you is that of general secretary, clerk typist, typist, or clerk. People with these competencies are excellent, but by definition they do not know what needs to be done next. They count on someone serving as their executive secretary, administrative assistant, or administrative coordinator to tell them what the next project is. Someone needs to lead them. That is you. Nevertheless, spend a modest amount of time in doing so. Do not turn yourself into an executive secretary who is supporting a clerk typist.

Clerk typists frequently teach ministers it is safer not to leave the office. Nothing gets done. The wrong things get done. The right things get done the wrong way. A clerk typist is glad for your company. They deliver positive reinforcement for your help. They thank you for being their executive secretary.

You have come to be a shepherd, not a secretary. Your focus is people, not paper. Yes, some paper may fall through the cracks. That is better than having some people fall through the cracks. Further, if you have a clerk typist who can grow her competencies, help her discover the training resources that are widely available in most communities. Encourage her to grow herself into an executive secretary, and then into an administrative assistant. But if you become the executive secretary, you block her growth. You have already filled the position.

Regrettably, a few pastors suffer from the disease of computerolatry. They are drawn to their computer. They are addicted to their computer. They sit in front of it day after day. They rationalize their behavior. They are not playing Freecell or solitaire; they are "working." Their clerk typist thanks them for all the paperwork they crank out—because the clerk typist does not have to do it. But in your new beginning, your best focus is with your people, not your office.

Remember you have come to be a good shepherd, a helpful preacher, a wise and caring leader, a community pastor. You have not come to be the church secretary. Mostly, you can do the 20 percenters that count in the first three months with modest secretarial support. Save for later the fuller development of secretarial support that helps advance the mission.

A fifth activity to save for later is *being somewhere else*. During this critical time of a new beginning, stay home. Oh, I do not mean that you postpone your vacation with your family. You will recall that Gene and the whole Welcome Team very much wanted their new pastor to take the vacation Marvin and his family had planned.

What I mean is this: give up outside denominational activities during this decisive three-month period. You may be on synod or conference committees. You may even be the chair of the group. You may be on regional or national committees for your denomination. You enjoy helping at the synod and national levels. You see good friends at the meetings. You enjoy contributing beyond the local church.

Tell whoever it is at the synod and national levels that you will see them in three months, that you are going to focus on your congregation for this new beginning time. Then, keep your word. Do not go to the meetings. Do not participate in synod, conference, regional, or national activities during this three-month period. Do not get sucked into doing synod or national business by phone, letter, or e-mail during this time. I do not care how important it might be. Teach your congregation you have come to love and lead them.

There are simply too many congregations where people sense that their new pastor is not "really there" during the beginning months. The consequence is that, in their minds, he never really gets there. The impression is created that synod, conference, and national activities are more important than the people in the congregation are. Stay home during this new beginning time. You will never have it again.

A sixth item to save for later is *debt reduction* or a *building campaign.* You want to begin as a shepherd, preacher, leader, and community pastor, not as a fundraiser. Your congregation, in earlier years, may have acquired debt as the result of a new building project or capital improvements to existing buildings. The leaders of the finance committee, deeply appreciative of the competencies you bring as their new pastor, approach you with the thought that now is the time to reduce the debt: "With the excitement of your coming, we are in the best position in years to really reduce the debt." Do not bite.

Debt reduction is the toughest way to raise money that I know of. Usually, we are asking a group of people who did not participate in the decision to acquire the debt to help us reduce the debt. People may have positive feelings about the building project or the capital-improvements program. Nonetheless, money to pay off a debt is tough money to raise. To be sure, the leaders of the finance committee may want to pursue a debt-reduction campaign. Given thoughtful consideration of all the factors, you may want to encourage them to do so. The best help you can give them is to focus on your shepherding, preaching, and leading.

If you allow yourself to drift into investing your time and energy in the campaign, what happens is that the campaign succeeds. I say the following gently. The campaign, if it is going to be successful, is likely to be successful anyway. However, by participating you are now stuck with the image of being primarily a fundraiser. It will take three years (usually the duration of the pledges) for you to come close to overcoming this image.

Essentially, the same principles apply to an emerging campaign for a new building or for capital improvements. You have not come to be the expert fundraiser. Encourage the building-fund committee. Share your wisdom and experience. Contribute your excellent ideas and good suggestions. Let the leaders of the campaign lead the campaign. Focus on your shepherding, preaching, and leading.

Indeed, your focus on shepherding does them more good than your going to the debt-reduction or building-fund campaign committee meetings. The spillover of your visiting with regular worshipers, shut-ins, and people in hospitals creates a grassroots impact of goodwill and positive reinforcement. More important, you are helping people with their lives.

A seventh project to save for later is *organizing the committees*. You will find that some of your committees are functioning well. Encourage them. Thank them. Leave them alone. Let them do their work. Some committees are on the borderline of being almost self-sufficient. Leave them alone. Let them find their own way to self-sufficiency. As a result, they have more ownership for their work. If you step in to help, they do not discover the deeper ownership for their work that makes them genuinely self-reliant.

If you invest your time with committees that are not quite functioning, you deliver positive reinforcement to negative behavior. The next best thing they can do is to not function again. You teach them that you will come running and deliver attention, affection, recognition, and dependency. They will continue not functioning.

Mostly, committees are made up of adults with some combination of strengths and competencies. Encourage them. Now and then, share an excellent idea or a good suggestion. Deliver positive reinforcement when, in fact, they do solid work. Never deliver false positive reinforcement. Do not create a codependent-dependent relationship with them. Let them find their best way forward. They will have high ownership for what they do. If you lead with these principles, a committee grows and develops. They deliver solid work that matches the competencies that they, not you, have. Sometimes, they discover that their competencies do not match the tasks of the committee, and they find their way to committees that match their gifts.

Some committees will not be functioning. Leave them alone. It is not accidental that they are not functioning. Their lack of functioning fulfills some purpose, some need. Competent people before you have sought to make them functioning committees. For whatever reasons, their efforts did not work. Indeed, it may in the short run be beneficial that these committees are not functioning. They may have been doing more damage than good.

You have come to lead a congregation, not a set of committees. You have come to help people with their search for community, not committee. Early on, though, someone will come to you asking that you get these nonfunctioning committees up and running. Do not bite. Stick to your shepherding, preaching, leading, and being a community pastor. Gently focus people on these key objectives. Let them know you are saving the functional committees until later.

In your congregation are both formal and informal leaders. Learn as much as you can about both. With committees, you only learn the former. If you invest your time primarily with committees, you miss many of the key leaders of the congregation. The informal leaders are as consequential as the formal leaders, if not more so. As you do your shepherding with your regular worshipers, you discover both the grassroots, informal leaders of the congregation as well as the formal, committee leaders.

There are two organizational "charts" in a congregation. One is the formal committee structure chart. The other is the chart of the informal, relational network of groupings. The leaders of the informal groupings are not necessarily also the leaders of the committees. Sometimes, there is little connection between the two. Sometimes, the overlap is modest.

In major decisions, the informal groupings decide the matter. They come out of the woodwork to support a worthwhile cause or defeat one they are not yet ready to do. They vote with their money and with their feet. They rally to a people-centered mission. They are less interested in some functional, institutional structural proposal.

Try not to call committee meetings early on. You are simply asking for trouble. You create the impression that you have come to be an administrator and a manager, not a shepherd and a leader. Let whatever committees plan to meet go ahead and meet. You are welcome to visit briefly, if you so desire, to share your words of encouragement and to come to know the people, as persons, more fully. Then leave.

If you stay, you find yourself involved in issues you do not understand, issues that have a long history, with many nuances and variables. Mostly, these are minor issues. They do not substantively advance the health of the congregation. You will be asked your opinion. Regrettably, eager to help, you give it. Thereby you use up some of your early credibility and leadership power on a minor matter, one that is not ultimately consequential. You walk into a low-key family feud you do not understand, on which you take sides, even though you do not even know there are sides or who is on which side. People play the "mother-father" game with you, and you are not even aware it is happening. You allow yourself to get caught up in a minor matter.

In this new beginning, focus on the important matters of shepherding, preaching, leading, and serving the community. Gene and the Welcome Team counted on their new pastor *not* to participate in committee meetings during the first three months. You can work out a comparable pattern with your Welcome Team.

Let the work of the committees move forward in whatever ways they can with your generous, thoughtful encouragement. You might attend one or two key meetings, but do not begin the practice of attending all committee meetings. You simply create codependent-dependent committees. Moreover, you lose substantial amounts of time you could invest in shepherding and being with your family. Focus where you can distinctively help.

AA groups, community groups, civic groups, quilt groups, interest groups, recreational groups, study groups, and many more all demonstrate the capacity to do solid work. They do so without the benefit of having a professional leading them, holding their hand, or giving them lots of advice. They do credible work, contribute to the betterment of the community, and advance people's lives. You want the committees of your congregation to develop the same spirit of self-sufficiency and self-reliance.

A wise, caring leader is one who leads with wisdom and compassion, not power and authority. With wisdom, you share solid vision, reasonable judgement, and common sense. With compassion, you share grace, caring, and encouragement. You help your people discover power, community, meaning, and hope in their lives in the grace of God.

People follow a shepherd, not a manager. People already have plenty of managers in their lives. They long for a shepherd. You are not here to be preoccupied with rules and regulations, conditions and situations, policies and procedures. Indeed, effective managers first establish grassroots, shepherding relationships with the team. MBWA—management by walking around—is, at heart, a grassroots way of developing relationships with the people on the team. The leader who walks the floor with wisdom and compassion creates a stronger team than the leader who stays in the office. Your "floor" is the people and the community you serve, not the church building in which you have an office.

People follow a shepherd, not a boss. You are not here to be preoccupied with power and authority, position and status, leverage and influence. Nor are you here to be an enabler—preoccupied with multiple processes of planning and excessive consensus building. Nor are you here to be a charismatic inspirer—preoccupied with one apocalyptic event after another, and seeking to be the savior in each traumatic crisis.

You are here to lead. My book *Effective Church Leadership* shares seven ways in which you can grow forward leadership in your congregation and community. In *Twelve Keys for Living*, the chapter on leadership helps in growing forward your own leadership of yourself.

Balance breeds balance. Excess breeds excess. Lead with a sense of balance. Your leadership stirs your people's best leadership. Focus on future, not past. Be at peace. Be not anxious. Share a relaxed spirit of leadership. Your spirit stirs your creativity and the creativity of your people. They have confidence that you lead with a wise, caring spirit.

A wise, caring leader does three things well: loving, listening, and leading. These three are good friends. It is not that they happen sequentially. They happen simultaneously. To be sure, in the early days of your new beginning, focus on loving and listening with your people. As you love and listen, lead. Listening and acting are not either-or. They go together. Loving and listening help you in your leading.

# 7

# Being a Community Pastor

We were having breakfast together at the hotel where I was staying. I was leading a national event that week for a particular denomination. We were having an extraordinarily good time together. People were very generous with me.

Dan asked if he and I could have breakfast together. Several months before the national event, we visited by telephone. He was going to serve a new congregation and he wanted to talk with me before he arrived at his new congregation. He wanted some ideas on what to do in the early weeks. I shared with him essentially the suggestions you are discovering in this book. We then agreed to have a meal together at the national event some months down the road.

Dan is a genuinely competent pastor. He carries his tall, lanky frame in an easy manner. His spirit is sincere and kindhearted, gentle and calm. He is not boisterous and loud. The weathering on his face comes from the days he worked outside before entering the ministry. He meets people graciously and quietly. He is not showy and overbearing. He is almost shy in his manner. He loves to have fun. He enjoys people.

My memory is that we gathered at the hotel restaurant on Thursday of that week. The hostess seated us at our table and left a menu with each of us. Almost immediately, even before the server could come to take our order, with a ring of wonderful astonishment in his voice and a look of bewildered, appreciative amazement on his face, Dan blurted out: "Dr. Callahan, I find myself helping people who are not part of my congregation. Help me to understand what is going on."

He was glad—indeed, he was pleased and delighted—to be helpful, but in his previous pastorates he had not experienced so many people in the community inviting him to be their pastor.

He went on to describe his new congregation. In the several months he had been there, he had come to love them, and they had come to love him. They were having a good time together. His Welcome Team was most helpful. Early on, he visited his regular worshipers, mostly where they work. He met many of the people with whom his members work.

At some of the workplaces, he heard appreciative remarks that he was there, since no pastor had been there before, and they were glad he was taking an interest in them. He visited the congregation's shut-ins, and he made it a point to visit with people in the hospital. Further, at the invitation of some of his members, he spoke to several community groups.

When I suggested these possibilities to him in our earlier telephone conversation, he was glad to do them. He found the Welcome Team especially helpful to him. He focused on his shepherding, his preaching, and being a wise, caring leader. He was surprised at the response from his congregation. They were more generous and gracious than he could have imagined. The congregation received him and his family with remarkable kindness and warmth.

Even more surprising, he was amazed at the response in the community. Several people in the community asked him to visit a loved one or friend in the hospital. Leaders of a number of community gatherings invited him to be part of the gathering. Several couples asked him to serve as pastor of their weddings. He served as the pastor of several funerals, and the families were most appreciative of his ministry with them.

He went on, at breakfast, to say that he was glad to help with these requests, that somehow they seemed natural in his new community. He did not think the requests were overwhelming. There were not that many. But it seemed as though there were slightly more requests than was true in his previous congregations.

He found himself serving as a pastor with the community as well as with the congregation. He was pleased with the emerging relationships with families in the community. He discovered that he understood his congregation better by coming to understand the community. Previously, his focus had been primarily inside his congregation. He was enjoying this new experience.

## A Mission Field

In our time, many people do not have a pastor. When a friend or loved one is in the hospital, they do not have a pastor to visit with them. When, because of some trouble in life or in their family, there is need for the wisdom, the compassion, and the listening ear of a pastor, they do not have one to call. In the time of a wedding or a funeral, they do not naturally have a minister to help with these decisive events in life. At the birth of a baby, or the celebration of a graduation, they do not have a pastor to celebrate these rich, full events with them.

In an earlier time, many people had a pastor. In the churched culture of the 1940s and 1950s, it was the thing to do to go to church, and lots of people went to church. As a consequence, they had a pastor. Thus, when events in their lives called for a pastor, they naturally turned to the pastor of the congregation in which they were active participants.

This is an age of mission. This is no longer Christendom. This is no longer a churched culture. This is one of the richest mission fields on the planet. In some communities, 70 percent of the population is unchurched. In some, it is higher. In a few communities, it may be somewhat lower.

When I knock on a door, and someone comes to the door and says, "Oh, well, we are Southern Baptist," I know immediately that they are unchurched. Be at peace. You will see it. Any Southern Baptist worth his or her salt who is active in a congregation usually says, "Oh, we go to the First Baptist. Brother Jimmy is our pastor."

When people give you a denominational label but do not identify a church or a pastor, they are teaching you one of two things. They are teaching you the church of their childhood memories. Or they are teaching you the church where they have an affiliation and are not active. Indeed, in our time, we are not working with people to get them back to church. We are now working with people who have never been there to come back.

In that long-ago churched culture, there was a concern that we not steal other church's members. There was much discussion about not proselytizing from other congregations. That made sense then, and it makes sense now. The difference between then and now is that in our time the majority of people do not actively participate in a congregation. Thus, there is less probability, when a person or family invites you to serve as their pastor, that they are active in another church. The higher probability is that they have heard of you on the community grapevine, and, having no pastor, have come to you for help.

"The day of the professional minister is over. The day of the missionary pastor has come." These words begin my book *Effective Church Leadership*. You will find the book helpful in discovering how a missionary pastor thinks, behaves, and lives. In your early weeks, you, like Dan, can have the fun of learning to think, behave, and act like a community pastor, not a professional minister.

Regrettably, professional ministers counted on a churched culture to deliver people to them. They waited on people to find them. They did not seek them out. Their focus was inside the church. They behaved and acted and—most especially— thought in inside-the-church ways.

Professional ministers graduated from seminary with two questions: Where is my office? When is my first committee meeting? This inside focus worked when the churched culture delivered people to the church. What you can count on and depend upon in our time is that the culture no longer delivers people to the church. The two leading questions of an age of mission are: Who is our mission? Who is our mission team?

You can count on these three things in your new congregation. One, there is a shortage of personnel and leaders. Two, there are inadequate supplies and funding. Three, there is hardly enough of anything. Be at peace. Healthy congregations are always giving away more than they have.

Like the missionary pastors across the history of the Christian movement, compassionate and competent, we deliver competent missional care in people's lives and destinies in the name of Christ. We do it well. God delivers strengths sufficient unto the mission. The stronger the mission, the greater the strengths God delivers.

The church was born in a manger, on a mission field. The church was not born in a mansion, in a churched culture. In its bones, the church knows it is most at home in an age of mission. We know, in our hearts, that we belong on a mission field. Only a few people lament, bemoan, and whine because God gives us the front lines of a mission field. Only a few long for a return of a churched culture.

Most of us, though, in our better moments, are wise enough to know that the church is not at its best in a churched culture. To be sure, in a churched culture the church enjoys the perks and the prerogatives, the prestige and the pedestal, but it feels ill at ease. We know we do not belong in that setting. There the church becomes bloated and bureaucratic, lazy and indifferent. On a mission field, the church is at its blazing best. There the church is lean and intentional, serving with compassion and hope.

You can train yourself to be a pastor in the community, not just in the church. You may have been trained to think inside the church. You can learn to think of the community as a whole. You can teach yourself to think, behave, and act as a community pastor.

In your new beginning time, accomplish two objectives as a community pastor. First, begin to *live out your longings to help*. Intentionally discover three to five families in the community you can help in one-time, gracious ways. Second, begin to *learn the mission field God has given you*. Purposefully seek out and develop relationships with some of the community centers and community groupings God has planted all around you.

You could also achieve a third objective. Encourage and invite your congregation to *look two to five years ahead* with these questions: "Who is our mission? Who is God inviting us to serve in mission?" However, I encourage you to focus on the first two objectives before you spend much time on the third.

Intentionally, help a few families in the community. Begin

to learn the community centers of your town. In so doing you demonstrate your own personal, practical interest in serving as a community pastor. You walk the walk, not simply talk the talk. You do what you are inviting others to do. Further, the third objective is no longer simply an intellectual exercise for you. It now has flesh and bones, people-pictures and reality to it. You begin to live out, in beginning ways, the question, "Who is our mission?" When you begin to live it out, then you are in a stronger, wiser position to ask it.

To be sure, early on, you have your best chance to gather your key leaders and the grassroots members of your congregation to look in missional ways at the coming two to five years. You can focus on a theology of mission, not a theology of maintenance. You can discover some of the 20 percenters in the mission to which God is inviting you. Begin with a search for mission, not a preoccupation with maintenance, membership, and money.

Begin by teaching your people, in this early time, by your actions and behavior, that you are a community pastor. If you do not teach them in this early time that you are a community pastor, they assume you have come to be an inside-the-church pastor. They have seen these pastors before. This is likely to be what they have learned to expect. But if, later on, you begin to do things in the community, they will be puzzled, perhaps even surprised and disturbed. You did not teach them the pattern of a community pastor in your early weeks and months.

Teach them, by your actions and behavior, not your words, who you are—a community pastor—and where you are headed; teach them that you look forward to serving God's mission in this community. With encouragement and grace, wisdom and experience, lead them to the community, so that together you serve God's mission well.

# Longings

Each of us has longings to help. God plants these longings in our hearts. We are drawn to serve, not survive. We want our lives to count in some worthwhile way. We know we are put here for a purpose. Among the gifts with which God blesses us are our longings to be helpful with people in their lives. Discover ways of helping that match the longings and strengths God gives you.

Some of us have a longing to share with those who have lost a loved one. Some have a yearning and gift to help people and their families who wrestle with alcohol. Some of us have a longing to help preschool families. Some have a desire to help youth. Some have a longing to help homeless persons. Some of us want to help others discover Christ.

Our longings tend to focus on

- A specific human hurt and hope, such as addiction, loss of a loved one, self-esteem
- A life stage, such as preschool, junior high, early retirement
- A community interest or concern, such as education, safety, jobs
- Helping people discover Christ, for the first time, or in deeper, fuller ways

Frequently, our longings focus on some combination of these possibilities. For example, I know several groups who have longings to help preschool families as they make the transition from preschool to elementary school. This is one of the very toughest life stage transitions. In our time, it is a transition equal to midlife crisis or early retirement. In the midst of helping with this transition, these groups find themselves involved in strengthening the quality of education in their community.

As another example, I am aware of a number of groups whose longing is to help youth who wrestle with alcoholism. In the process of helping, these groups find it is important to help young people discover a power higher than themselves, and to invite them to discover the grace and compassion of Christ. They also develop a concern to have an impact, at least a modest one, on the cultural norms regarding alcohol in their communities.

You discover your own longings to help as you think about the times when you have genuine fun in helping someone. This spirit of fun is trying to teach you your longings. What we have fun doing is God's way of teaching us both our longings and our strengths. God gives us longings to help concretely with specific human hurts and hopes, and God gives us competencies sufficient unto our longings.

You discover your longings as you consider the times you lie awake at night worrying over some person and the dilemma with which she is struggling. Your worries over that person are trying to teach you your longings. You discover them in thinking of the times when you are driving down the road, and your mind keeps drifting to an individual or family wrestling with some problem in their life. The drifting in your mind is trying to teach you your longings. Or notice the times when you feel a deep satisfaction in helping someone. This sense of deep satisfaction is trying to teach you your longings.

We bring to a new beginning—whether to a new congregation, or a present congregation—our own deepest longings and best competencies. We begin at our best when we begin with God. It works less well to start a new beginning without God. Some ministers allow themselves to become so distracted with busyness and fluff in their early weeks and months of a new pastorate that they live those early weeks and months virtually without God.

When you live out your longings and competencies to help in the early weeks and months, you begin with God. You begin your new pastorate with the gifts God gives you. If you deny your strengths, you deny God's gifts. If you claim your strengths, you claim God's gifts. You begin with God.

The simplest, most helpful way forward is for you to discover some one-time possibilities where you can live out your deepest longings and best competencies with several people in the community. Yes, you will be helpful with people in the congregation. It is equally important that you live out some of your longings in your community.

God invites us to a theology of service, not a theology of survival. Some congregations become preoccupied with a theology of survival. They live in a frame of mind and perspective of retrenching, retreating, and trying to avoid losing more than they have already lost. It is very easy to allow yourself to get caught up in this frame of mind, this perspective.

From the first day of your new beginning, view yourself as a pastor with the community as well as with the congregation. It is not helpful to work from the premise that once you get things organized in the church you can then do something in the community. That day never comes. Or it will happen so far down the road that you will develop amnesia over your longings to help people in the community. In the early weeks and months, live out your longings and competencies in simple, one-time, helpful ways in the community. You avoid getting caught up in a theology of survival, and by your helpful actions and behavior, you teach a theology of service.

## One-Time Ways of Helping

Live out your longings to help in simple, one-time ways. Specifically, in your early weeks and months, discover three to five families in the community. I am not suggesting you seek out twenty or thirty. That would be too many. In fact, if we begin to think of twenty or thirty, we end up doing nothing in the community. We think about doing too much, so we end up doing nothing. We postpone action to postpone failure.

I am not suggesting that, at the outset, you get caught up in lengthy planning sessions based on demographics, charts, and statistics. There is time enough for those things later. With the help of your Welcome Team, simply identify three to five families that match your longings and competencies. Seek these families out. In one-time ways, be helpful with them in their lives.

There are three reasons.

## Helping Families

First, you are helping these families in the community. You enrich and strengthen their lives with your compassion and hope, your wisdom and experience. Your help is simple and direct, gracious and thoughtful. Your help is an act of encouragement, an act of neighborly helpfulness.

Look for simple possibilities. For example, you might discover someone in the community, perhaps a friend or relative of someone in your congregation, who is in the hospital. In a one-time visit, share the generosity of your grace and your compassion. With the help of your Welcome Team, you might discover someone in the community who is celebrating a special birthday, or a couple celebrating a special anniversary. In a one-time, celebratory spirit, share a shepherding visit to congratulate them. You might find a teacher who is a legend in a nearby school. Simply have lunch with her, coming to know her and sharing your spirit of encouragement with her.

What you are doing is finding several families in the community with whom you share a genuine interest in them and their lives. It is not so much that you are problem hunting to do problem solving. You do not need to cast yourself as the solver of people's problems. There are plenty of people around like that.

What you do is share with them a word of encouragement. There is much discouragement in this life. There is genuine grace in sharing the gift, the grace of encouragement. Your encouragement is, with them, a simple act of generosity. It helps them on their way in this life's journey.

The art is to deliver just enough help to be helpful, but not so much help that the help is harmful. One of the mistakes those of us who seek to be helpful make is that we deliver more help than is helpful. The help becomes harmful and creates a pattern of codependency and dependency. By contrast, a simple act of generosity is a genuine gift of helpfulness.

At this point, you need not become involved in long-term counseling or in-depth therapeutic care. With some people, you can share the gift of referral. Your Welcome Team can help you know who, in the community, is excellent in long-term counseling. In your new beginning, someone may present himself to you who would benefit from long-term counseling. The best help you can give them is to refer them to some competent resource person in the community.

You may have a major gift, competency, or long-term experience in the field of in-depth, therapeutic counseling. Investing considerable time in counseling might make sense for you to consider—later on. In your early weeks and months, you want to get to know as many people as possible in the community and the congregation. Doing weekly counseling with one or more individuals severely limits the amount of time you have available to get to know people and families.

Sometimes, pastors who allow themselves to be involved early on in long-term counseling discover—later—that the person is also seeing someone else. What happens is that the person has doubled up on therapeutic resourcing. One of your best gifts of helping is referral. Thus, in your new beginning, focus on simple acts of kindness and generosity. Share them with a few people in your community.

## Communicating with the Congregation

Second, you are communicating to your congregation that you have come to be a community pastor. As you help these few families in the community, you teach your congregation, in the simplest way possible—by example—that you have come to be a pastor in the community, not just inside the church. It helps, early on, if you affirm to your congregation that you look forward to being a missionary, shepherding pastor in the community.

Intellectually, congregations know this. Emotionally, congregations hope for pastors who serve the whole community. At the same time, a few congregations think that help should begin at home, meaning that pastors should first look after the church that "pays his salary." In fact, we pay the salary so that the pastor will serve the community as well as the congregation.

When John Wesley made his helpful statement, he did not say, "The church is my parish." His statement was quite clear: "The world is my parish." Both congregations and pastors can deepen their understanding of this truth. When you help three to five families in the community—one family in each of your first three to five weeks there—you advance this process forward.

In one congregation, the chair of the finance committee, the chair of the council, and a key leader insisted that the primary focus of the pastor's work in the first few months must be inside the church. They felt there were so many things that needed tending inside the church. They wanted the focus to

be on the administrative, organizational, and financial problems of the church. They felt that their new pastor would
have no time to help families in the community. They suggested this point even before the pastor came to serve the
new congregation.

Halfway through the first three months, the sister of the
finance committee chair went to the hospital. She was not a
member of any church. The chairperson counted on his pastor
to visit. At about the same time, the wife of a nephew of the
personnel committee chair gave birth. They were not members of any church. The chair counted on his pastor to be helpful. Additionally, the key leader called to ask if the new pastor
could conduct his aunt's funeral. She was not a member.

With each of these people, the message seemed to be "We
want you to focus only on people in the church—except
where our families and friends are involved; then we count
on you to be a community pastor." The truth is people do—in
their bones—want you to be a pastor in the whole community, not exclusively with the congregation.

We can study missions. We can hold committee meetings
about missions. We can plan missions. The simple way to
teach missions is to put on the grapevine that you have come
to be a pastor in the community—not just in the church. You
send this message as you graciously and gently help three to
five families in the community in your early time. These families benefit from your help. You don't have to say anything
about it. The grapevine teaches the message for you.

## Communicating with the Community
Third, you are communicating to the community that you
have come to be a community pastor. By your actions with
these three to five community families, you teach the town
that you have come to be a pastor in the community, not just

inside the church. As you help these families in the community, you share the message that you see your task as shepherding with the whole community, not just inside the institution.

Mostly, the help you share with these three to five families is what I call next-door helping. It is made up of gestures of kindness and caring. It is the kind of helping that good neighbors share. It is help through simple acts of sharing compassion, encouragement, and hope.

The apostle Paul writes, "Be ye therefore transformed by the renewing of your mind." It is not the deepening of one's commitment. It is not rising to the challenge. It is not working longer and harder hours. "Be ye therefore transformed by the renewing of your mind" has this helpful insight: how we think shapes the way we behave; how we behave shapes the future we create.

If you think of yourself as a community pastor, you behave as a community pastor, and you create a future of being among the legendary community pastors in the area. If you think this way, you seek out persons whom God has planted all around you, and you share help in neighborly, next-door, one-time acts of grace and encouragement.

I do not know how to explain this precisely to you. You will find these people, and they will find you. Sometimes, it is as simple as walking next door and visiting with whoever lives where you are now living. Sometimes, it is walking next door to the businesses around your church, if your church happens to be in a business area.

One year, I was leading a seminar in New Zealand for a large number of congregations. We were meeting in one church. During the morning break, I walked next door to the butcher shop specifically to visit with the person who owned the shop. Before him, his father and his grandfather had owned this same shop. During the twenty-five years that this person owned and ran the butcher shop, no minister had ever gone there. We had a good conversation that morning.

I make it a practice to go next door and visit. I'm amazed at how many ministers have never been just next door. I look forward to coming to know who is working in what shop within the immediate area of our church location. I have fun beginning to know some of the families who live in the general vicinity of the church.

I was helping in one congregation, and the pastor, Sam, and I decided that we would do some visiting late that afternoon. We needed to be back in time for the Wednesday night supper at the church. He wanted my help in learning more fully how to visit.

As we got into his car, I asked him where we were headed. We were headed, he said, way down the road to visit a specific family. I knew it would take most of our time to get there and back, and we would have very little time for a visit with that family.

I said, "Why don't we visit some of the people in the immediate area of the church? We'll have more time, and we can share in more visits."

He said, "Oh, I've already visited all the members around the church."

I said, "That's fine. We can simply visit with some of the people who live around the church who are not members. Let's visit with the people who live in that yellow house."

He said, "Oh, is there a house there?"

His selective perception worked so well that he only saw the houses of his members. He could tell me where each of them lived. However, he hardly even saw the other houses around.

He kept driving.

I said, "Let's try that gray house."

He kept driving.

I said, "Well, let's try this house up ahead on the road. There's a sign out front indicating this person does hairdressing for people in this rural area. This will be a good house to visit. I'll bet she keeps up with what's happening with families in the community."

He pulled his blue Volkswagen over to the side of the road, and with his hands clenching the steering wheel, said, "I can't visit people I don't already know. I don't know her. She hasn't been to my church."

I said, "That's fine. I'll take the lead."

Sam said, "But you are not from around here."

I said, "That's fine, I'll take the lead. We'll have a good visit."

We had a good visit with her. She appreciated our coming. In the visit with her, we discovered she did more than hairdressing. We learned of her gentle spirit and her gracious manner. She shared something about the families living in the area. It turned out that she served as an informal mentor and shepherd with many of the women in the community. Much more happens in a hairdressing shop than hairdressing. She had grown up in the area, and she was kind enough to share with us some of the history of the area. In doing so, she remarked that we were the first pastors who had ever visited with her.

Sam's congregation was seeking to serve children and their families. We asked her to share one or two excellent ideas she thought would be helpful. She did. One of her ideas was so good that it eventually became the focus of the congregation's mission with children and their families. She brought us tea, or coffee, or water. It may even have been apple cider; at this point, I do not remember which. What I do remember is that as we were leaving, she gently touched each of us on the arm, and looking at Sam she said in a hopeful whisper, "Thank you for coming. Come again."

We went on to visit several other families in the area that afternoon.

We were not doing program pushing or membership hustling. We were simply sharing genuine visits of shepherding, having an interest in people and their lives, giving them a word of encouragement and helping them sense the grace of God. We had fun that afternoon. We had interesting conversations with people. It is amazing what people share with you about their lives if they are given half a chance.

Early in your new beginning, discover a few community families and share simple acts of next-door helping. For healthy congregations, their perspective is in the community, not solely inside the congregation. Healthy congregations count on you to serve the congregation and the community. Unhealthy congregations have the assumption that they pay you to serve only inside the congregation. You deepen the health of your congregation as you teach them that you have come to be a community pastor.

## Community Centers

Intentionally seek out some of the community groupings, both formal and informal, that God has planted around you. With the help of your Welcome Team, select five to eight community events that help you come to know the community better. Participate in several one-time events important to the community. Go to a high school football game. Attend a community music event. Visit the centers of the community. Learn the mission field God gives you.

To be sure, you are learning your community as you visit with your regular worshipers where they work. As you visit with them, you are also visiting some of the centers of your community. As you speak to several community groups, you are also learning about the centers of community life.

With the help of your Welcome Team, look at the various centers of community life. See which ones you discover as you visit with your regular worshipers and as you speak to several community groups. Then, consider which additional centers of community life you would have fun coming to know. With your Welcome Team, discover how, in one-time visits, you can begin to learn of these centers.

Some of the centers of a community are

vocational, professional

sociological, ethnic

geographical, neighborhood

human hurt, hope

life stage

civic, community

hobbies, interests

arts, music

educational

retired

political, governmental

recreational

business

religious

Look for and listen for the informal relational groupings in the community. Some community centers are formal and institutional. Some are informal and relational. You will find a fuller discussion of this in *Twelve Keys for Living: Possibilities for a Whole, Healthy Life*, in the chapter on community. For the moment, I simply want to confirm that these groupings, whether formal or informal, have these significant characteristics:

- A set of goals and values
- A set of customs, habits, and traditions
- A communication network and language dialect
- A leader or leadership, authority, and decision-making process
- A sacred place of meeting (sometimes multiple places)
- A common, shared vision of the future

Each community grouping has its own sense of these qualities. You can begin to discover the centers or groupings that are decisive in your community. Look for the ones that are constructive and helpful.

One decisive center in many communities is the educational center. You may have already visited with a regular worshiper who is a legendary teacher in an elementary school. In this one visit, you accomplish two possibilities. You visit with one of your regular worshipers. You also begin to discover the educational center of the community.

Sometimes you may not have a member who is part of the educational center. That's fine. Pick the educational center that is legendary. Visit with one or two of the leaders in this educational enterprise. Get to know them. Study the strengths and competencies they have. Learn the dilemmas with which they wrestle and puzzle in everyday life. Invite them to share with you their wisdom and experience. Begin a relationship of mutual interests and possibilities.

As you visit with your regular worshipers where they work, you are visiting some of the vocational centers of your community. It may be a textile mill, a manufacturing plant, a bank, a gas station, a construction company, or a service business. Sometimes, a vocational center may interest you, but you may have no regular worshipers there. Nonetheless, you can visit and get to know some of the leaders there. Perhaps no pastor before you has visited there. Perhaps no pastor following you ever will. You will have fun. You will learn about your mission field.

Visit with one or two civic and community groups. Look for the ones that are considered to be among the constructive, helpful groups in the community. You do not need to join them. Simply share a one-time visit. Begin to discover some of the goals and values, some of the customs, habits, and traditions with which they live through life. Learn about the common, shared vision of the future that they contribute to the community.

Think of your own hobbies and interests. You may enjoy art or football, music or golf, quilting or basketball. Seek out a grouping in the community that matches your hobby or interest. Visit them one time. You do not have to join. Simply have fun getting to know some of the people with whom you share a common interest.

I encourage you not to put this one off "until I get settled." You will get caught up in the busyness and the business of your church. Time passes. You postpone. You say to yourself, *Well, after I get things straightened out in the church, then I will visit with that group.* Time passes. Amnesia sets in. You forget. One of the best visits you can make in your early time is with a group that shares a mutual hobby or interest with you.

As you learn about your community, you learn about your congregation. The two go together. Your community influences your congregation as much as your congregation influences your community. As you learn of the centers of community life, you are also learning about the centers of life in your congregation.

I was helping one congregation in a county seat. The members were known for their feuding and fussing with one another. They seemed to stumble continually into some spat or fuss. The grapevine would buzz. Groups would argue. Unsigned letters would arrive. Meetings would last long into the night; then they would have to stand around in the parking lot until eleven-thirty making up.

At the next meeting, the fuss would start up again. Angry words would be exchanged. Bickering and backbiting would be plentiful. Sometimes, shouting would happen. After a time, they would get tired of that fight. The novelty would wear off. Then, there would be a time of truce and resting up, as they got ready for the next fuss.

Asa gives the Bible study in the men's bible class on the first Sunday of each month. Junior gives the rebuttal on the third Sunday of each month. There are neutral teachers on the second and fourth Sundays.

Asa's great-great-grandfather pioneered in the area, and Asa's wealth is in the land, the farms, and the timber. Junior's great-grandfather came later, and the focus of Junior's wealth is in the town and the shops. Asa is chairman of the board of First Bank. Junior is president of the *new* bank, which was founded thirty years ago.

Asa is active in Kiwanis. Junior is active in Rotary. Asa elects the county sheriff. Junior elects the mayor. Asa owns the Chevrolet dealership. Junior owns the Ford dealership. You can almost tell who is in which cell (which significant community grouping) by the kind of car he or she drives.

It is a two-cell town. Therefore, it is a two-cell church. Sometimes, when you learn the community you understand better the patterns that are happening in your church. The congregation frequently reflects the dynamics of the community.

The pastor of that congregation was wrestling with the periodic fusses and fights that happened in his church. The dilemmas of serving the church became difficult for him. He invited me to come and help puzzle it through. He knew my own writings and work well enough to understand that he was working with a two-cell church.

Among the things that two-cell churches do best is fighting. It is the fight between the Old-timers and the Newcomers. Now, the Newcomers are not that new; they came thirty years ago. But from the perspective of the Old-timers, they are new.

The arguments are endless. Someone has moved the kitchen utensils from where they have always been. A particular sign has always been this way. We always do homecoming that way. We do vacation Bible school this way. The newsletter and the bulletin have always looked like that. Sometimes, they even forget what they are fighting about.

I invested several days with the pastor and the congregation. I helped the pastor understand more fully that he was not dealing with simply a two-cell church. It was a two-cell town. The thing a two-cell town does best is fight. Some of the fights were spilling over into the church.

A friend of mine was instrumental in opening the old Sunbeam plant in that county. I happened to be there on the day the plant was opening. It would deliver 150 new jobs. That is considerable for such a town.

We were standing in a circle: Asa, the pastor, Junior, the new plant manager, my good friend who was opening the plant, and I. Asa and Junior were sharing with the manager and my good friend that they would be happy to loan whatever money would help the business move forward. They were continuing to compete in their two-cell way.

Following the opening ceremony, I said to the minister, "Invite the new manager of the plant to teach the young couples' Sunday school class that you are starting in a few weeks."

He looked puzzled.

I said, "Yes, I talked with the manager. They have moved to this state to be closer to her parents in their old age. They were active in their previous church. He taught Sunday school there. If you were to gently invite him, he would be glad to teach the new young couples' class in your church."

I went on to observe, "You have now become a three-cell town. The manager is the leader of the third cell. Given half a chance, with him teaching the young couples' class, you will become a three-cell church."

The solution to a two-cell fight is to grow a third group. Three-cell churches still fight, but they take turns. They fight around. Two-cell churches fight incessantly. Three-cell churches begin to find whole, healthy ways forward.

What is happening in your church is not happening just there. What is happening in your church is directly related to what is happening in your community. Therefore, it becomes important to discover the community centers and groupings and to have some sense of how their dynamics influence the dynamics in your congregation.

As you become a community pastor, you help people with their lives, you understand your congregation more fully, and you influence your community in healthy ways.

# 8

# Having Fun

G ene and the Welcome Team did excellent work here. In the early gathering with their new minister and his wife, the team discovered some of the activities Marvin and his family enjoyed doing for fun. Then they worked out several fun activities that matched the interests of Marvin, Murlene, and their two sons.

The Welcome Team's central emphasis was on Marvin and his family as persons. Their focus was relational and congregational, not functional and institutional. The spirit of Gene's team was focused on the congregation as a family. The emphasis was not on the minister as a role or the church as an organization.

They wanted the congregation to be a welcoming family with Marvin, Murlene, and their children. They did not want to leave their new minister and his wife to fend for themselves in this early time. They wanted to be open and inclusive, warm and welcoming. They did not want to come off as closed, exclusive, clannish, and cliquish. They wanted to share gestures of hospitality and welcome.

Sue gathered two fun outings for Marvin and his family, one in July and one in August. The first outing, to which Sue invited three families whose children were of a similar age, was a picnic at a nearby park, known for its lake, walking trails, open green spaces to play, and gardens of flowers. The second outing was a day at an amusement park with three other families. Both were fun outings for all.

Ben arranged for Marvin to play golf with three other people at the golf course at which many of the congregation played. He also worked it out for Marvin, who enjoyed speaking, to speak to three community groups: a civic group in July, a parent-teachers group in August, and a recreational group in September. Janet arranged for Murlene, along with several women of the congregation, to attend a community music event together.

Ben, Sue, and Janet each had a get-together, one per month, at their respective homes in July, August, and September. They specifically invited friends who were not members of their church. Each get-together was an opportunity for people in the wider community to come to know Marvin and Murlene, and for both of them to begin getting to know a range of people in the wider community.

These events grew out of that early conversation. They tailored the events specifically to the interests of Marvin, Murlene, and their children. They consulted with Marvin as they developed the events. They wanted their new minister and his family to feel at home and to have some fun in their early months. The new pastoral family, the Welcome Team, and the congregation shared grand, good, fun times together.

## Relax

The player who goes to the plate with a relaxed intentionality tends to get on base. The player who goes to the plate determined to hit a home run on every pitch does one thing well: he strikes out. I have never said to one of my players as he goes to the plate to take his turn at bat, "Be sure to hit a home run." What I say is, "Have fun." People do better when they are relaxed and having fun.

At the end of many sports events, the announcer asks the person or team that won, "What is your secret? What did you do differently this time?" Most frequently, the response is, "I decided to relax and have fun."

Note that they do not say, "I decided I needed to try real hard to relax." The harder we try to relax, the tenser and tighter we become. The art of relaxing is to loosen up. It is less a matter of trying to relax and more a matter of letting go, of deciding to ease off. If you can discern the difference between needs and wants, it is easier to relax.

The more relaxed you are, the more relaxed your congregation is. The tenser and tighter you are, the tenser and tighter your congregation is. The more nervous and anxious you are, the more nervous and anxious they are. Tense and tight, nervous and anxious pastors and congregations do not do well together.

One of the difficulties with congregations is that in fact they allow themselves to become too tense and tight. Some have been that way for years. It is not accidental that they experience a declining pattern. The more declining they become, the more nervous and anxious they are.

In your new beginning, share good fun with your family. Whether with a new congregation or your present one, in your first three days, three weeks, three months, relax, have fun, be at peace, and enjoy life. Live in Christ.

To this point in the book, I have encouraged you to be a good shepherd, a helpful preacher, a wise and caring leader, and to begin being a community pastor. I have also suggested several activities that you can save for later. Now we discuss your relaxing and having fun. I have purposely put this discussion before the chapters on discovering and growing the team and developing your future. I encourage you to have fun with your family. A few pastors are tempted, regrettably, to become busy growing the team and developing the future. A rush of excitement comes with a new beginning.

The temptation is to focus on the institutional and organizational future of the church, to get caught up in one meeting after another, one project after another, one new program after another. People in the congregation get caught up in this same rush of enthusiasm. In meeting after meeting, the pastor and the people reinforce one another. Frequently, the result is a neglect of oneself and one's family.

Having fun with your family is a higher priority than growing the team and developing your future. In fact, if you make it a point to relax and have fun with your family, you are likely, later on, to grow the team and develop your future more easily. In this new beginning, you have the chance for a new beginning with your family as well. It is a rare opportunity. I encourage you to take advantage of it.

Frequently, I serve as consultant helping congregations and ministers who have become tense and tight, nervous and anxious. In a good spirit, I note that if being tense and tight were going to work, it would have worked by now. They have invested considerable energy and time in this course of action, almost assuming that if only they try harder, things will get better. The truth is that the harder we try, the tireder we are, and the tenser and tighter we become. We continue to decline.

It is simply this. People are not eager to become part of a group that is tense and tight, nervous and anxious. They already have enough groups like that in their lives. People long for, look for, a group that is relaxed. They know, instinctively, that they will learn how to relax in such a group. Thus a new beginning is a time for relaxing and celebrating. This is a time for joy and laughter.

I encourage many congregations to share together in a "year of celebration." Let your first year be a year of relaxing and having fun together. We can celebrate

- The life God grants us
- The strengths God gives us
- The mission to which God invites us
- The compassion with which God surrounds us
- The family and congregation with whom we find home
- The hope with which God leads us

We celebrate more than the fact that we have a new congregation, or that we have a new pastor. We rejoice in who we are and whose we are. In a relaxing, good-fun spirit, we share a wonderful year of celebrating and discovering, relaxing and having fun.

Across your first year, have the fun of several major celebrations together. Ah, yes, our first Sunday together can be one of those celebrations. Your installation as the new pastor is important. We do more than simply recognize and welcome you as the new pastor. On this day, together, as congregation and pastor, we consecrate our lives, our strengths, our mission, our compassion, and our hope. We covenant to be family together, living in the grace of God. We become pastor and congregation in a new beginning, full of promise and hope.

During our first year, we can share in a homecoming Sunday in September. We can celebrate our first Christmas together. We can rejoice in our first Easter together. We can discover one or two other celebrations that make this a wonderful, relaxing year together. At the end of our first year, we can have a remarkable concluding celebration, looking forward to many years together.

Each of these major celebrations can be our gift to the whole community. Each celebration can have a team. The team achieves two objectives: integrity and invitation. They plan the integrity of the event. They invite the community to participate. Through direct mail, personal notes, personal telephone calls, and personal visits, they actively extend invitations to the whole community. Because of the team's leadership, we will have the best Christmas ever. The same will be true of Easter. Indeed, these several major celebrations across the year give us our best year ever.

We only have this first year one time. We will never have it again. We could make the mistake of becoming tense and tight, nervous and anxious. We could become preoccupied with the problems, needs, concerns, weaknesses, and shortcomings with which we are faced. Instead, we choose the wiser course. We relax and rejoice. We celebrate our being together.

The problems, however minor or major, that are present in your congregation have been there for some time. Long before you arrived. You did not create them. Other people brought them into being. You did nothing to contribute to these problems. Regrettably, the quicker you become preoccupied with these problems, the sooner they become *your* problems. Leave them alone, for now.

This is not the time to play fix-it. This is not the time to be the answer person. This is not the time to play you-have-a-problem-and-I-have-the-solution. In your desire to be helpful, you may be drawn to that temptation. But this is not the time to fix things.

This is the time to relax. This is the time to focus on people, not problems. The problems come to you soon enough. Get to know your people. Get to know your family deeply, fully. Do so in a relaxed, easy-going spirit.

# Have Fun

Have fun with your family. Do not imagine you can get every-thing organized and then, once you have things organized, spend time with your family. You will never spend time with your family because you will never get everything organized. Have fun with your family in the first three days . . . the first three weeks . . . and the first three months.

Your family needs your love and care, your laughter and good fun. You need your family's love and care as well. Mutu-ally, you and your family discover richer, fuller ways to have fun together. You are a more helpful pastor as you share your love and care with your family and, equally important, as you benefit from their love and caring, their joy and laughter.

In this new beginning, focus on some of your *favorite activities* as a family. You can plan some of them together. You can give each person in the family the chance to select sev-eral favorite activities that the family will enjoy sharing together. Moreover, you can encourage each person in your family to participate in several activities he or she enjoys doing individually.

This new beginning is an excellent time to have fun with your favorite activities, before everyone gets caught up in busy, hectic schedules. You may enjoy sports, music, quilting, hiking, art, sightseeing trips, camping, sailing, and more. Intentionally select and share a number of favorite activities in which you have fun. Invite your Welcome Team to share their knowledge of the local area. Further, they will be glad to sug-gest possibilities you may not think of. As with Gene and his Welcome Team, they may even help you plan some of them.

Take your *vacation*. If you have planned a vacation before coming to your new congregation, feel free to have fun on it. Gene's team encouraged Marvin to do so. Remember that

Ben said, "I want us to start September with a rested quarterback, not a tired one."

This is a special vacation. It is the first one you are taking from your new home. This does not suggest that you use it to travel around and learn your new area. Rather, it means that a move creates an even more intense longing for roots, place, and belonging. A move is a time of dislocation and discovery, of lostness and newfound hopes. Packing and unpacking boxes is fun *and* fatiguing. The vacation does you good. You are more rested and relaxed.

Have fun on your *day off*. In your previous congregation, or in recent years in your present one, you may have taught yourself how not to have a day off. Your intentions to take a day off were good, but something always seemed to come up. The day off was lost.

Now is the time to focus on your family. You can change that old pattern. In your schedule, you can be faithful to both yourself and your family with your days off. Think of the day as a fun day, as a family day, as a rest day, rather than a day off. With "day off," there are vague pictures. With fun, family, and rest, we have concrete pictures.

I learned a helpful way to ensure that I take my family day. Originally, in my date book I simply drew a line through the day I planned to take off. The result was that I hardly ever got my fun day. It would elude me. Inevitably, something "important" came up and I allowed whatever it was to change my plans for my rest day.

I learned to be as specific about this day as I was about every day. I quit drawing a line through that day in my calendar. The line was not specific enough. The thing that came up *was* specific, so I did it and lost my day off. I learned to schedule my day off intentionally with specific activities. I now get my family day.

I encourage you to be deliberate about how you plan activities for your day off. Schedule how you plan to use it: for fun, family, rest, and yes, some chores. Write in your calendar for your day off in given week: "Take Johnny fishing; catch four fish." You will take your day off, you will take Johnny fishing, and you may catch some fish. "Take Julie shopping. Go out to eat. Have fun at the movies." Now, you will have your day off.

As you take your days off, and have fun with them, your sermons are more helpful and less challenging. Your sermons are more insightful and less a call to commitment. Your sermons are not dull and boring. They are not strident and demanding. You have fun with your preaching because you are having fun with your life. Your sermons are helpful and hopeful, stirring and inspiring. Your sermons have a spirit of compassion and a sense of community.

Have fun with *special holidays*. During this time of new beginnings, several special holidays come along. Depending on the season of the year, they may be Labor Day, Independence Day, Memorial Day, and so on. You will discover a variety of local as well as national holidays. Enjoy them with your family. Do not use them to catch up on things at the office. Do something for fun with your family.

When Jesus is asked what the Kingdom of God is like, he describes the kingdom as a wedding feast, as a great banquet. The kingdom is not solemn and stern, dull and dreary. It is a gathering of joy and wonder, laughter and good fun. In this spirit, share good fun and good times with your family in your new beginning. Have a spirit of fun in all you do in your first three months, and in your first year.

Some of us need to learn the art of having fun. On occasion, I say to someone, "Share with me what you have fun doing." There is a blank stare, a puzzled look. This is a new question for some of us. We have not thought in these terms.

We are serious and solemn, dedicated and committed. We went through college and seminary. We studied hard. We made

good grades. We accomplished much. We did so in a determined, driven spirit. We turned each good, fun time that came
our way into a work project. The focus was on attainments,
accomplishments, and achievements. There was no time for
fun. We had too much to do.

Some of us are still learning to have fun. It may be something we missed learning in our growing-up years. We had
too much to do. In your new beginning, purposefully, look for
people in the congregation who know how to have fun. They
are legendary for their capacity to have fun in life. Spend time
with them. Have fun with them. They help you and your
family have fun. You learn the art of having fun.

Have a grand honeymoon in your early time with your
congregation. Celebrate and rejoice. Share in many fun times
together. Enjoy a remarkable and memorable year of fun and
celebration. Yes, some people talk about a time when the
honeymoon is over. Some pastors never get to the honeymoon. They immediately become too preoccupied with the
problems and challenges. The more joyous and wondrous the
honeymoon, the more likely you will get through the tough
times ahead.

## Be at Peace

When you arrive at your new congregation, you may tell
yourself that this is going to be "a real opportunity," "a really
interesting venture." You may discover there are more problems here than you were led to believe. In meeting someone
new, most of us put our best foot forward. We do not immediately focus on our difficulties and problems. Sometimes, it is
because of this that we do not learn of the problems sooner.

Sometimes, a congregation is eager to secure a minister as
competent as you are. They may not have had a minister
as capable as you in some years. They may make light of some

of their problems. In their enthusiasm for your coming, they may understate the severity of their difficulties. Wishful thinking sets in. They assume that with your presence, the problems will either not matter so much, or that you and they together can quickly solve them.

I honor that a few congregations intentionally mislead a new pastor. They consciously hide some of their problems out of fear that they will not get a competent pastor. They deliberately misstate key facts, having to do with the state of their finances, the quality of their staff, or the range of volunteers they have. They lie about their membership figures and their worship attendance.

If this should happen to you, know that you are dealing with a pattern of behavior that is likely to have been in place for a long, long time. As best you can, try not to take it personally. You will probably discover that the grassroots congregation is as much in the dark as you were. More often than not, it is only a few leaders who engage in this pattern of behavior. You are not the first person with whom these lies have been shared.

Certainly, you want to make a clear assessment of your options. You want to consider what, in fact, makes sense for the future. As you do so, I encourage you consciously to spend more time with your family. Their love and support helps you. Your love and support is important to them. It is not pleasant to discover one has been lied to. Such a situation shakes our faith in the decency and honor of people. Perhaps you move to this new congregation only to discover the membership is not there, the worship attendance figures are inflated, and the money is gone.

We rush here and there. Our resentment and anger grow. We become withdrawn. We make hurried, foolish statements. We take people to task. We become passive, and our preaching becomes dull and boring. We become aggressive, and our preaching becomes grim and strident. Nothing seems to work. Naïve idealism creeps in. Depression joins us. Despair comes along. Dependency tries to take hold. We are not at our best.

Be at peace.

This is not the first time in our lives that we have been lied to. In the end, the issue is not that we have been lied to. That has happened before. It will happen again. The issue is how we deal with what has happened. We cannot control other people such that they will never lie again. We can control how we behave in relation to other people. We cannot control them. We can control us.

We can chart a course of integrity and honesty, dignity and honor. We can know that most people and most congregations seek to do likewise. Across the years, I have found only a few leaders of congregations who misstate the facts. Most leaders and congregations seek to do the right thing. They cherish their honor and honesty, their integrity and their word.

More often than not, when you discover problems that you were not told about, it is not because the leaders and congregation have intentionally lied to you. It is because they have lived with their problems so long that they hardly notice them. It is like a spot of mud on a windshield. We are driving along, having fun. The car ahead of us, or a car passing, kicks up a bit of mud that lands squarely in the middle of the windshield, on the driver's side. It is right in the center of our view. For whatever reason, the windshield wipers cannot dislodge it.

We continue driving, staring at it. It is annoying. It blocks our view. We try the windshield wipers again. We use the washer water. We try the wipers again. Nothing works. We are in a hurry. We keep driving. Time passes. After awhile, we do not notice the mud spot. It is as though we learn to look around it and beyond it. It simply becomes part of the scenery.

Sometimes, congregations do not mention some of their problems for the same reason. They have lived with them so long that they no longer notice them. They look around and beyond them. The problems have become a part of the scenery. Selective perception has come into play. It is almost as if they do not know the problems are still there.

The irony is that many of these disappearing problems can be solved in a straightforward fashion. But simply because you, as a newcomer, can see the problems—and even the solutions—does not mean that you should now become busy fixing them. Save them for later.

My wisest counsel to you is to be at peace. Encourage in yourself a spirit of serenity. Invite God to help you:

*Accept the things you cannot change*

*Save for later some of the things you can change*

*Have the wisdom to know which changes will make
a difference*

*And live in the grace of God*

Some congregations are essentially healthy, even as they may have several, or even a number of, problems. The only people I know who do not have problems are the people buried at the nearest cemetery. Sometimes, I am not so sure about them. When I walk by late at night, I hear the mutterings and the murmurings. Whole, healthy people have problems. It is not the absence of problems that makes us whole and healthy. It is the presence of strengths for living that help us have the capacity to solve some of our problems and have the ability to live beyond the rest of them.

The same is true with congregations.

Strong, healthy congregations have problems. They are healthy because their strengths and competencies are present.

In *Twelve Keys to an Effective Church*, I discuss the twelve strengths that are persistently present in effective congregations. Healthy congregations have nine of the twelve well in place. For one congregation, it is a certain nine. For another congregation, it will be another nine. The art is to grow forward the nine that best match the strengths God gives you and the community in which God places you.

It is helpful to be at peace about the other three that are not well in place. One of two things happens with them. The first possibility is that the congregation delivers so well the nine that match that the other three do not matter. The second is that a spillover impact takes place. By delivering well the nine that match the congregation, some of the other three may come along on their own.

Healthy congregations have confidence in their strengths. Given a limited amount of time, energy, and resources, they choose, wisely, to build and advance their strengths. They do not spend their limited resources of volunteers and money on the problems that in the end do not advance their strengths. They know, with assurance, that when their strengths are well in place they live effectively and fully in God's mission. They have confidence that they can be whole and healthy, knowing they have the capacity to solve some of their problems and the ability to live beyond the rest.

Sometimes, we get caught up in the problems and miss the strengths. We are eager to help. We want to be useful. We are glad to be here. We want to show our appreciation. Our compulsion toward perfectionism takes over. We want everything to be perfect. We want to do our part. We begin to tackle problems that do not matter. We try to solve too much too soon. Frustration sets in. Impatience follows. Depression joins us. We imagine the honeymoon is over.

The truth is that we have allowed ourselves to become the victim of our own compulsion toward perfectionism. We have missed the point that some of these problems have been around for years and, more important, that their presence has not deterred the congregation from being whole and healthy, effective and confident.

Sometimes, both our compulsion toward perfectionism and our sense of betrayal join forces. We want things to be "nearly perfect." We have high expectations. Our enthusiasm is bubbling. We arrive. We discover some problems we were not told about in advance. We feel we have been misled. We feel we have been suckered in. We feel disillusioned. We feel betrayed.

We do not like to feel betrayed. We imagine that by solving the problems so that they are no longer present, we will not feel so betrayed. Their presence reminds us of our feelings of betrayal. We think that once they are gone, we will no longer have feelings of betrayal.

Be at peace. Progress is more helpful than perfectionism. Live one day at a time. Grant yourself what God grants you: a spirit of serenity. Why withhold from yourself what God gives you? Know that some problems do not need to be solved now. Know that some problems do not need to be solved ever. In the whole design of things, they do not matter that much. Practice the peace you invite others to have. Accept the serenity God gives you.

## Enjoy Life

Enjoy life. We get to live this life once. God gives us an amazing gift—the gift of life. We might never have been born. We might never have been alive. It is a remarkable miracle that we live and move. Our hearts beat, our lungs breathe. We think and feel, love and hope.

Life is a gift. It is not something we have earned. Life is not a possession that we somehow deserve. It is not inevitable, the automatic result of a mindless process, somehow mapped in genetics or written in the stars. The gift of life is not of our own doing; it is the gift of God. We can be grateful to God for this remarkable gift of life.

In our thankfulness and gratitude, we can enjoy the life we have been given. We do not need to spend the time we have in complaining and lamenting, bemoaning and whining. Life is short. We do not need to waste this precious gift in that manner. We can have a spirit of joy that we are, in fact, alive. We can enjoy whatever life we are given. We can thank God for this amazing gift.

We might as well enjoy this life. The choice is to decide to enjoy life or to decide not to enjoy life. We could decide to go through life with a glum, gloomy, downcast spirit. We could live with frown and fear. We could be worried, always preoc- cupied that we did the wrong thing way back when, that we missed our chance in the past. We could rehearse and repeat all of our imagined mistakes to whoever listens. Think how well you enjoy being around people who live life that way.

Now, think of the people you know who enjoy life, richly and fully. They endure hardships. Tough times come. Disap- pointment and defeat are present. Sickness and death intrude. They continue to live an abundant life. They do not deny the hardships and difficulties. They live with the capacity to deal with them. They do not allow them to control their lives. They live with a spirit of confidence and assurance. Yes, there are occasional doubts, fears, and dreads. But they continue to enjoy life.

People are drawn to those who are enjoying life. People are not drawn to a congregation of scribes and Pharisees, righteous and religious, feuding and fussing. People are al- ready in enough groups that bicker and fight; they do not plan to join yet another one. They look for others who are enjoying life.

You may discover you are the pastor of a *healthy, capable* congregation. Many congregations are solid and strong. Enjoy life with them.

A few pastors do not know what to do with a healthy congregation. They view themselves as problem solvers. They see their task as fixing problems. Then, when they find themselves serving an essentially healthy congregation, they do not know what to do. Almost without realizing it, they began to create problems so they have something to fix.

They are uncomfortable with health and wholeness. They are more at home with weakness and problems. They create just enough confusion and difficulties that they distract the congregation from its strengths. The congregation becomes preoccupied with its problems. Now, the minister is at home. He has something to fix.

Healthy congregations do have problems. No one does not. By focusing on our strengths, we put ourselves in a solid position to deal with our problems. If we claim our strengths, build on our strengths, do better what we do best, then we are in the strongest position to deal with our weaknesses. We also know that some problems are sufficiently minor that they are best left alone. Such problems do not matter that much. We invest our energies in building our strengths.

But a pastor who likes to fix problems gets a congregation away from its strengths. The congregation is now in the weakest position to deal with its weaknesses. In medicine, the focus used to be on illness and the sources of sickness. In recent times, there has emerged an emphasis on wellness and the sources of health. Wise pastors learn that "if it ain't broke, don't fix it." They learn that when something is working well, they do not try to fix it. They enjoy the gift of a whole, healthy congregation and give thanks to God.

On occasion, you may discover you are the pastor of a *troubled* congregation. The best thing to do is to focus on the present and the future, not the past. With the past, we can do two things. We can ask God's forgiveness for our sins of omission and commission. And we can give thanks to God for the accomplishments and achievements that have been. We cannot change what has been. We can do something with what now is and what can be. Find the one or two strengths your congregation uses well, and build the future on them.

Sometimes, you may discover that you are the pastor of a *declining or dying* congregation. Congregations do not die because the people in them are lazy and apathetic, indifferent, complacent, and unconcerned. Most declining congregations are blessed with a small group of people who are devoted and dedicated, working hard to avoid further decline. The problem is not that no one is committed. Usually, some are deeply committed. The problem is that they are working at the wrong things. They are working very hard at the things that worked forty years ago and no longer work.

Intuitively, they know this. They sense that those approaches so successful in bygone times have become dysfunctional. Regrettably, there are enough memories of long-lost success with these approaches that they continue to haunt us. Maybe, if only we try harder. . . . For the moment, give thanks to God that at least you have a few people who are willing to work hard. The art is to help your people discover how to focus their commitment and dedication on the things that work now.

Frequently, the hard workers develop a spirit of despair and defeat. The antidote to despair is not success, but joy. People have a better chance to move forward as they learn how to enjoy life. When you enjoy life, you help your congregation to enjoy life. If you allow their spirit of despair and defeat to overwhelm you, you lose the joy of living. Further, you confirm in them that the appropriate view of life is despair and defeat.

You may discover you are the pastor of a *two-cell* congregation. As we discussed in Chapter Seven, two-cell congregations frequently fight. They often do not even realize they are doing so—the pattern is so ingrained. In the heat of the battle, they say things they do not fully realize they are saying. This learned pattern of behavior is almost automatic. Regardless of the specific issue, they exchange the same rumors, words, and invective that they have tossed at one another in the midst of every fight in the past.

Each cell—the Old-timers and the Newcomers—seeks to draw you to their side. It is somewhat like a small town in the old west where a range war is raging between two ranchers—or, even tougher, between a rancher and a sheepherder.

A stranger rides into town, not aware a range war is consuming the area. He is just looking for a place to call home. Before he can even get off his horse, he is asked, "Which side are you on?" Innocently, he says, "What are the sides?" The answer comes terse and quick, "Stranger, if you don't know the sides and haven't chosen whose side you are on, ride out of town before sundown. We don't want you around."

Now, it is not quite this harsh in a two-cell church. What you do know is that some of your predecessors sided with the Old-timers, and some with the Newcomers. Some tried to straddle the fence and got shot at by both sides. Some left.

You are here. You can maintain some sense of your sanity, live your life with a spirit of joy and serenity, and—as best you can—have fun as you do *some* of the following:

- Have fun with your family. Strengthen your home life with good-time activities.

- Focus on a good-fun, one-time mission project. Help the community look beyond themselves.

- Focus on three, one-time, fun projects the community would enjoy doing.

- Do not take the fight personally. It has little to do with you. Do not be offended.
- Do not give offense. Keep your side of the street clean.
- Learn some of the old ghosts that are playing themselves out in the fight.
- Stick to balance. Balance breeds balance.
- Avoid excess. Excess breeds excess.
- Be at peace with yourself.
- Sense the grace of God in your life.

Do not get caught up in the fights. The kitchen fight (someone moved the kitchen utensils from where they have always been) was preceded by the table fight (someone moved the table at the back of the church). Every fight has its ancestors. Two-cell congregations usually find something about which to fight. Then they have a period of truce and resting up. Then they find something else to fight about. There is a pattern and rhythm to their behavior.

Being pastor of a two-cell church is not fun. Keep your perspective. You may benefit from reading the Al-Anon twelve-step book. It is a helpful resource for learning how to control one's own behavior in the midst of turmoil and addictive patterns. Do not allow yourself to be drawn into these fights, taking one side or the other. Worse yet, do not allow yourself to be drawn into being the umpire or the referee. You will simply be caught in the crossfire.

The way forward in a two-cell church is to grow a third group. A three-cell congregation still fights, but they take turns. The balance of power shifts. It is a whole lot easier to be a three-cell or four-cell congregation than it is to be a two-cell congregation. Your healthiest course of action is to began to develop a third cell. Take your time. Do it well. Do so with a spirit of joy and compassion, leadership and hope.

In your new beginning, whether the congregation is healthy, or troubled, or declining, or dying, or two-celled, you illustrate sound wisdom as you share by your example a spirit of enjoying life. You do not need to fall victim to naïve, whistling-in-the-dark, foolish idealism. This simply leads to cynicism. Nor do you need to fall victim to a down-in-the-dumps, defeatist attitude of despair. This yields depression and dependency. Rather, you can live and share a spirit that this life is worth living well.

Some people spend half their lives worrying about their problems and their death. The irony is that they might not even have been alive to worry. They waste their lives in worry. We might never have been born. We are indeed fortunate to be alive. God invites us to live an abundant life. Enjoy the life God gives you.

In this new beginning, have fun with your family. Get to know and love them more deeply and fully. Relax, have fun, be at peace, and enjoy life. Allow yourself to enjoy your life, your family, and your congregation. Celebrate this first year together. Enjoy your favorite activities, your vacation, and your days off. Enjoy the special holidays you celebrate with your family.

As you enjoy life, you see the way forward more easily and quickly. Be not tense and tight, nervous and anxious. Be at peace. We get to live this life once. Some people are already tense and tight enough. They do not need to see you becoming tense and tight as well. Being tense and tight has not helped them beyond their problems. Your joining them in their nervousness and anxiousness does not help.

You are here to love and lead. You are here to be in mission and to shepherd. Enjoy life. We are the Christmas people. We are the people of wonder and joy. We are the Easter people. We are the people of hope and new life. Enjoy the blessings God gives you. Have fun with your family in this new beginning. Let this be a time of new beginning with them.

# 9

# Discovering Your Team

Judy came as the new pastor in July, with the Welcome Team meeting her in advance. The team did excellent work in preparing for her coming. In July, August, and September, she focused on shepherding, preaching, leading, and coming to know the community as a pastor. In November, Judy would gather the congregation for a planning retreat.

Her early visits with regular worshipers, shut-ins, and hospital patients were better than she anticipated. She was having fun with her preaching. The feedback was that her sermons were helpful. She sought to be a wise, caring leader, and by and large she did well. She saved a number of lesser projects for later. She was learning her people and her new community. She made it a point to have fun with her family.

Several leaders urged her to have a planning retreat in August, virtually right after she came. They noted the genuine enthusiasm with which she had been received. Worship attendance was up. Giving was strong. They pointed to the fact that the church enjoyed the best July they had ever seen. They suggested that she build on this initial surge of participation; "strike while the iron is hot" is what one of them said.

Judy shared with them that she wanted, in her first several months, to learn about her people more fully before they held a planning retreat. She was wise enough to know that only by coming to know her people would she develop the discernment to discover the strengths and leadership possibilities they possessed. She wanted to focus first on her shepherding, preaching, leading, and coming to know the community. Early November made sense to her.

For the retreat, they would meet at a community center, known for its beauty and relaxing spirit. They discussed meeting for five planning sessions over five weeks at the church. This works well for many congregations, and as a result the congregations develop excellent objectives for their future. In the end, Judy and her steering team decided they would have the most fun doing their planning in an easy-going, pleasant retreat setting. They shared an open invitation with the whole congregation. Everyone was welcome.

They planned to have fun together on the retreat. They knew that people make better decisions if they are relaxed and having fun. People's energy levels are higher. Their creativity and anticipation levels are higher. Their anxiety levels are lower. So Judy and the team counted on the planning sessions themselves to have about them a spirit of good fun and celebration.

They began at six-thirty on Friday evening with an enjoyable dinner together, which led into their first planning session. They concluded at eight-thirty so they could share tea, coffee, and dessert while they visited with one another. They held their second and third sessions on Saturday morning, eight-thirty to ten, and ten-thirty to twelve. Over a wonderful, light lunch, they held the fourth planning session. Their fifth, wrap-up session was from one to two-thirty.

They decided on the few objectives to head toward. A good time was had by all. The grassroots people appreciated

being included in the retreat. There was broad-based ownership for the objectives they decided on. There was a spirit of
enthusiasm and encouragement. People looked forward to
the future.

Judy has been the pastor of this congregation for many
years now. She is a legend in the community. They look back
with appreciation for the way she put people before planning
in her early beginning. They are thankful for her discernment
in discovering the team. They are grateful for the objectives
they decided on that first November. Those few objectives set
them on a solid course. They have had many enjoyable planning retreats since.

## Discover the Team (Not the Dream)

Arnold began his early months by rushing into planning before
he got to know his people. He was in a hurry. Indeed, that
is what people remember about him. They say, "Arnold was
always in a hurry." He was decent enough, honest enough, but
he always seemed to be heading somewhere in a hurry.

Even before he arrived at his new church, he put in mo-
tion the plans for a series of cottage meetings. He wanted
them set up in advance, so he could begin doing them in his
first week. He wanted to meet with people in small groups to
discuss the church and its future. Initially, his leaders thought
this was a good idea. As it unfolded, they were less sure.

They anticipated that the cottage meetings would give
their new minister the opportunity to begin to know the people of the congregation, and for the congregation to begin to
know him. And, yes, in each cottage meeting Arnold did go
around the circle and give everyone a chance to introduce
themselves and share a brief word about their family. But his
spirit, in leading these introductions, was hurried and per-
functory. It was as if he wanted to get to the real business.

Quickly, as the introductions concluded, Arnold brought up what he called the central question for their future. He introduced the question in an enthusiastic, stimulating manner, saying, "If money were no object, what would your dreams be for our church?" The focus of each cottage meeting was virtually entirely on that question.

There was much excitement in the cottage meetings. Arnold seemed to know what he was talking about. They were glad he was asking them their opinions. Many suggestions poured forth. Much newsprint was used. The buzz on the community grapevine was of all the ideas that were brought up. A lengthy report was gathered. Committees were appointed.

However, deep down, what people learned in the cottage meetings was that Arnold was interested primarily in growing a bigger church. They were the stepping stones to that end. Regrettably, they learned, early on, that his interest in them was as a means to an end. Thus, when tough times came, the shepherding relations were not there. He moved on.

Now, Arnold was nice enough. He was courteous and kind. He was not mean or malicious. He was not anxious or angry. He liked the people in his congregation well enough. He simply had one goal: to become bigger. In a low-key, calculating manner, he did what he thought was necessary to achieve that goal.

I encourage you, in your early months and even in your planning, not to go near the question, "If money were no object, what would your dreams be for our church?" There are three dilemmas in the question: money, dreams, and church.

The question immediately reduces the whole matter to a consideration of *money.* People become concerned as to whether they have enough money. Healthy congregations never have enough money. They are always giving away more money than they have. They are always living at the edge of their resources for the sake of their mission. Money follows mission, not the reverse. God provides money sufficient unto the mission. The stronger the mission, the more generous the money.

The focus on *dreams* stirs compulsion toward perfectionism. Many of us have enough difficulty with that old friend. We do not need to begin our new future together by setting too many goals too high to be accomplished too soon. Regrettably, we gladly participate in such idealized brainstorming, knowing deep down that we have been on this path before and nothing came of it.

Sadly, the focus on the *church* in the question teaches people that the primary concern of the new pastor is on the future of the church rather than on the future of their lives. The question could have been, "If money were no object, what would your dreams be for your life and your family?" Although this question still has the problem of focusing on money and dreams, at least it focuses on the people. It demonstrates a genuine interest in their lives and their futures.

How you do your planning teaches people what you think of them. Judy began with the team. Arnold began with the dream. Judy is a legend. After a flurry of excitement, Arnold moved on. In growing your team, I encourage you to benefit from these four steps:

1. Discover your team.

2. Decide your objectives.

3. Structure your team.

4. Coach your team.

Put first things first. Focus on the first two steps before you focus on the last two. Discover the team God gives you.

Discover the objectives to which God invites you. Then you can structure and coach your team. We can structure the team once we know the objectives. We can develop the objectives once we know the team.

## Where to Look

The first step in growing your team is to discover your team. Look for the team God gives you. Look for the team you really have, not the one you wish you had. You cannot grow a team you have not taken time to discover. You cannot discover objectives in midair. You discover objectives in relation to the strengths of the team you have.

We match the plays with the players. We send in plays the players can run. We do not send in plays the players cannot run. We do not send in plays we think the players *should* run. We do not send in more plays than the players can run. We send in plays the players can run. This takes knowing the team.

Look for the groups God gives you. Then, look for the competencies these groups bring to the mission. God gives you seven groupings of people who can be part of the mission, who can be part of the team:

- Regular worshipers
- Staff
- Constituents
- People served in mission
- People in the community
- Friends of the church who live elsewhere
- Members

### Worshipers

We have already discussed regular worshipers. I would simply add that in your visiting with them you are both beginning a shepherding relationship and discovering the strengths of some of your team.

## Staff

Staff are a significant part of any congregational team. Staff may be volunteer, part-time, or full-time. Volunteer staff do not receive pay but function very much as part of the staff team. Likely, they are members of your congregation; at the same time, they develop an identity as part of the staff. Jill has been giving three hours a day on Monday, Wednesday, and Friday, volunteering in the church office. She has been doing this for years. She does it because, years ago, the pastor was helpful to her niece who came to live with Jill. Her niece had come for a "visit" lasting the final five months of her pregnancy. She gave birth to a baby boy. During the whole time, Jill's pastor was helpful, gracious, and caring. He was the shepherd who was with them during the months of pregnancy. He was at the hospital early that Tuesday morning when Joshua was born. He helped in the months that followed. Jill never forgot his shepherding. For her, volunteering in the office was the least she could contribute in gratitude. She was part of the staff team.

Some congregations have a one-person staff, namely, the minister. Some have a modest staff including a minister, a volunteer or part-time choir director, perhaps a secretary, and someone who does custodial work. Some congregations have considerable staff to advance the mission they share in the community.

## Constituents

Constituents are nonmembers who participate in some program or activity in your congregation. Their participation is frequently in the one-time, seasonal, and short-term events that your congregation offers. Sometimes, they are part of your weekly, monthly, or year-round activities. For example, they may be part of your seasonal vacation Bible school, or your ongoing preschool.

They may participate in your seasonal basketball, soccer, or baseball teams, or they may be part of your regular youth or adult groups. They may share in specific, major annual events and mission projects, or they may participate regularly in a Bible study group, a prayer group, or an interest group. They may sing in a special musical event each year, or they may be regular members of a choir.

Many constituents see themselves as members. They discover help, hope, and home with this congregation. They give of their strengths and their generosity. They see themselves as part of the family. They do not understand our neat, tidy distinction of formal membership. Informally, by their participation they think of themselves as part of the congregation. They see themselves as part of the team.

## People Served

People served in mission are those your congregation has helped directly in recent years. The help may relate to some life event or human hurt or hope important to that person and family. They may have been helped with a hospital visit, a wedding, the birth of a child, a baptism, a celebratory event, a funeral, or some other significant event. It may be that your congregation has helped them wrestle with some problem, such as addiction, dependency, or grieving. Your congregation may have provided resources for a given life stage, such as preschool, youth, or early retirement.

People served in mission are glad to help your congregation—with a mission that matches their strengths, builds on how they were helped, and has a one-time or seasonal spirit to the project.

They are not interested in regular committee work. They share generously with you in some project that helps people in the community. They help in the way they were helped. They can be an important part of your team.

## People in the Community

People in the community think well of the mission of your congregation and are, from time to time, glad to be of help. The Salvation Army draws on many people in the community in its mission with the poor. Young Life does the same in its mission with youth. Habitat for Humanity constructs many of the homes it builds with the support of those in the community.

If your congregation (1) has a compelling mission and (2) asks with confidence and assurance, then many people in the community respond and share their competencies and generosity with you to help advance your mission. If a congregation does not have a compelling mission and does not ask, but instead primarily looks to its own members for sole support, then those in the community do not respond. They can respond if you ask them. In our time, many community people are happy to help with a worthwhile project.

## Friends of the Church

Friends of the church who live elsewhere can be a helpful part of your team. They may have grown up in the congregation and now live somewhere else. They may have been active during the time they lived in your community. They may have been married in your church, or shared in some other major life event in your congregation. For whatever reason, they look to your congregation as having been especially important to them at some point in their lives.

Develop a specific project that matches their interests. If you ask, they will share the generosity of their giving to help advance the project. Plan a specific weekend or weeklong mission project in your community. Some of them will come to help you, just as people do when they go on a work project in Appalachia or the Caribbean.

### Members

Members are those people who have decided, at some point in the past, to join your church through its formal procedure. They may come now and then. They do not participate frequently enough to be considered regular worshipers. They share their strengths and generosity from time to time. Their participation may range from moderately active to occasionally participating.

## Mission and Team

All seven of these groups are helpful to the mission of your congregation. The art is to discover the project that resonates with a specific group, and to invite them, with wisdom and integrity, to share their competencies and generosity. If you stir their spirit of compassion and their sense of community, they will be part of the team.

Note that I list "members" last among the seven groups. There are two reasons. First, I want you to see that God gives you all seven groups, not just members. If you look only at your members for help with the mission, you miss many of the people who are glad to help. You limit the strengths of your team to the competencies in your members and miss the considerable competencies and strengths available to you through some of the other groups.

Second, and perhaps more important, I want you to know that people respond to the value of the mission project and to the integrity of the invitation. The mistake a few ministers make is to assume that because someone is a member he should respond, regardless of how vague the project may be. The appeal is often that he simply has a responsibility to do his share because he is a member.

However, the appeal to "remember your membership vows" is not compelling. People do not do what they do because they are members. Indeed, one has to wonder whether we want people to do what they do in God's mission out of obligation and duty. The apostle Paul suggests that "God loves a cheerful giver." In the same spirit, I think God loves a cheerful volunteer.

We do what we do with a spirit of gratitude for God's blessings in our lives. We share our competencies and strengths with a sense of generosity for the grace with which God blesses us. However, a member who shares her competencies and generosity out of duty and obligation becomes, finally, a reluctant participant on the team. Her contribution is half-hearted. Her guilt grows. Her interest withers. Eventually, she will do what she does—if anything out of law rather than grace.

When you stir the interests of members, you do so on the same basis as you do with any of the groups. You share the value of the project with a compelling compassion and a strong hope. You share your invitation with integrity, confidence, and wisdom. People respond. They do so with a spirit of grace.

You will note that I have not included inactive members in the list of groups with which to build your team. Someone may suggest that you visit inactives in your early months, or in a new start in a present congregation. I encourage you to save for later any preoccupation with inactives. One of the mistakes congregations make is encouraging a new pastor immediately to contact all the inactives in the church. The assumption is that now that we have a new pastor, the inactives may become active.

Save inactives for a later time. In the end, there is no such thing as an inactive member. For whatever reasons, they did not find a sense of community here with us. They are not inactive and somehow waiting at home for us to show up. Sometime ago, they began actively to search for a sense of belonging somewhere else. They may have already found it. It may be in a church, an interest group, a recreational group, a civic group, a vocational group, or a service group.

Most people become inactive because something simple interrupts their pattern of participation, and no one notices. To be sure, we remember well the person who leaves in a huff, angry and upset. Perhaps 10 percent of people leave in that highly visible way. We remember them because of the storm of their leaving. The vast majority of inactives leave for less-conspicuous reasons. Something happens in some area of their lives—perhaps the illness of a parent or relative, a death in the family in another community—and no one notices.

Harry and Arta were active in their congregation. They participated in many of the projects. They gave amply of their competencies and their generosity. They were good members. Arta's aunt became ill in a nearby city. On weekends, Harry and Arta went to visit. They were there for the surgery. It did not work, but she lingered long. She was beloved of them. They spent more weekends there. She died.

They served as the administrators of the estate. They were there more weekends. There was the house to go through, the boxes to be unpacked and then packed again. There were the treasured articles and belongings to send to various people in the family, and the house to sell.

The pastor and congregation were dimly aware that all of this was happening, but no one knew the aunt. Besides, all of this was going on somewhere else, in another city. No one helped Harry and Arta directly with their grieving. But Harry and Arta did not live in that other city; they lived here. Their grief was here, even as the events with Arta's aunt happened elsewhere. Harry and Arta had been active in their church, but no one noticed their grief. Slowly, Harry and Arta slid into the woodwork and became inactive.

The company promoted Steve to a new job. It meant traveling during the week, and sometimes on the weekend. People in the congregation were glad for Steve with his new promotion. His travel meant that some of the chores he used to do during the week now had to be crammed into the weekend. The stress of his new job was more than he anticipated. No one really shepherded him during this time. He began to come less frequently to church, and, finally, slid into the woodwork.

As I suggested in Chapter Three, visiting and shepherding with regular worshipers, the congregation's shut-ins, and with people in the hospital is like junior high and high school ball. Helping inactives become active again is like super pro ball. We have taught them, over a number of years, that we are not in a shepherding relation with them. It takes a number of contacts to help them know that we, in fact, are genuinely interested in them. Thus, I encourage you to save inactives for a later time.

Focus for now on discovering the team God gives you among your regular worshipers, staff, constituents, people served in mission, people in the community, friends of the church who live elsewhere, and members.

## What to Look for

Knowing where to look is helpful. Knowing what to look for is decisive. When you assess the gifts that people bring with them, look for these strengths:

- Competencies
- Compassion
- Commitment
- Leadership qualities
- Team ability
- Integrity
- Growth

## Competencies

Discover the groups God gives you; then assess the competencies present among people in these groups. Do so with wisdom, not wishfulness, and accuracy, not idealism. Two mistakes often happen in assessing the competencies present in a congregation. First, we look for the strengths we wish were there. In our wistful wishing, in our naïve idealism, we try to find the strengths we hope are there, the ones that match our own preferences and choices. However, you are looking for the competencies that are present, not the ones you wish were present.

Second, in some congregations, the pastor and leaders look for whoever is willing. They feel desperate for volunteers, so they take anyone who comes forward. Thus, what frequently happens is that willing people end up in a project that does not match the gifts they have. Intuitively, they know the match is not working. They try harder, and fail yet more miserably. They try again, and learn again that the match is not working. Their discouragement and depression cause them to miss the real competencies they do have.

You are looking for who can do it well, not who is willing. Some people are willing to volunteer for almost any project, but this does not mean they have the competencies that match the project. The biblical principle is that there is a diversity of gifts. Not everyone has gifts to do everything. We all have been given specific gifts that enable us to help in specific ways. You are looking for those with solid competencies that match particular objectives to advance the mission.

Look for both the specific and general competencies that people have, and that they bring to the mission. To discover specific competencies, decide which distinctive assets are directly helpful to the objectives of the task. Then look for excellent matches.

In visiting, you are looking for people who have the capacity to listen well. In finance, you want people who have the gift of growing generous givers. In recreation, you are looking for people who have skill in that sport. In worship leadership, you want people who have a sense of presence, who have solid delivery, and whose words have helpful content.

When looking for someone to work with youth, it helps to know the young people with whom the person will be working. Some youths have a strong athletic orientation. Some have an intellectual, or extracurricular, or social, or fad-of-the-moment, or outcast, or independent orientation.

In one congregation, the leaders in the church school described to me the discipline problems that a particular teacher was having with a junior high class. I visited with the teacher and discovered she had excellent competencies to work with young people who have a strong intellectual orientation. The difficulty was that most of the youths in her class had a strong athletic orientation. The discipline dilemma, therefore, was the kids' way of trying to teach her they did not learn in the way she taught. With a different teacher whose specific competency was an athletic orientation, the discipline problem disappeared.

We discovered another group that had a strong intellectual orientation. We matched the first teacher with that group. She flourished. The group flourished. Much learning took place because of the excellent match.

To discover general competencies, decide the fundamental assets you hope each person brings to the leadership task. Think through the basic, foundational elements that you count on each person having well in place.

Look for wisdom and experience. Yes, I encourage you to be willing to work with those who have beginning wisdom and experience. However, it helps to distinguish between enthusiasm and wisdom. Some people bring wonderful enthusiasm to the task, but I learned long ago not to allow their enthusiasm to convince me that they have wisdom. What they have is enthusiasm. This is fine in a beginning leadership task. If the task is more advanced, look for wisdom and experience.

Look for people who know how to work hard without making it look hard. Some people take a simple project and make it look hard. They lament and complain. They call attention to "everything I'm doing." On the other hand, some people take a complex, difficult project and move forward with grace and ease. They focus on the end result, not on what they are doing to get there. They expend considerable effort, but they do so with a relaxed pace that helps the rest of the team. Look for them.

Look for people who are on time in achieving their objective. I do not mean that they are on time at meetings. Being on time at meetings is helpful, but this is not a matter of punctuality at gatherings. It is that they plan to achieve a certain objective by a specific date, and they do so. Certain people are on time for meetings. They are, in that sense, punctual, but they bring with them their excuses as to why they have not achieved their objective. They teach the rest of the team that they do not really plan to accomplish their objective. They consume the time of the meeting with their laments and complaints. It is refreshing to discover people who say they plan to achieve an objective by a certain date and who successfully do so. Look for them.

Look for those who have learned the capacity for creativity and flexibility. They know how to learn from both their mistakes and their achievements. They listen well. They draw on the resources of their mentors. They demonstrate their ability to think and behave in new, creative ways. They know their own mind, and they have the confidence and assurance to discover new possibilities. They are not tied to customs, habits, and traditions that worked in an earlier time.

If they have grandchildren, I look for how they relate to them. When I see that they are open and flexible, generous and accommodating with the grandchildren, I have the sense they will be likewise with the team. They look for new possibilities. They try new ways. They will bring a fresh flexibility to the task and the team.

## Compassion

Look for the compassion that people have, that they bring to the mission. Ask yourself whether they have a compelling passion for the mission at hand. Do they have a deep love for people? Do they know how to work with and get along with people? Are they growing in their people skills? Is their compassion rich and full, rather than codependent—dependent in spirit? Do they know how to share help with wisdom and discernment, or do they have a tendency to give more help than is needed?

Finally, we are in a people business. We are not in an industrial, manufacturing business. We do not produce so many widgets per year, with quarterly profit-and-loss statements. We are not in a church-growth business where the bottom line is so many new members and so much new money per year. We are invited to serve, to not be preoccupied with our own success. God encourages us to a theology of serving, not surviving. God invites us to have the same rich, full compassion with the people we help that God shares with us. With this spirit of compassion, we encourage people to live whole, healthy lives in the grace of God.

## Commitment

Look for the commitment people have. You are looking for people who have a commitment to the specific mission of your congregation. This is important. The church that tries to help everybody with everything ends up helping nobody with anything. Such a church attains the mediocre middle in all it does. It squanders its resources in too many directions. People who have a commitment to everything have, finally, a commitment to nothing. You are looking for people who can *focus* their commitment with excellence.

The Salvation Army has a specific mission to serve the poor. It lives out this definitive commitment in all it does. It focuses its leadership, volunteers, and resources on serving this distinctive mission. It shares the "blood" of compassion and the "fire" of community to serve the poor. People who become part of the Salvation Army have a matching commitment.

You may decide the specific, primary mission to which God invites you is one with children and their families. This matches both the strengths of your congregation and the community around you that has a high density of families with children. Someone may come to your congregation with an enthusiastic commitment to single young adults, or to senior adults. Their enthusiasm causes them to *insist* that this become the primary mission of your congregation. They have a strong commitment, but it does not match the mission to which your congregation is committed.

One possibility is for their commitment to be expressed as a secondary priority in your congregation. It is like college.

Something is the major. There are also minors and electives. However, they may *insist* appealingly and persuasively, or insistently and dogmatically, that their priority must become the major priority of your congregation. The best solution is probably for them to express their interest in some other group or congregation whose specific mission matches their interest.

You want people who have a commitment both to the mission and the team that is present in your congregation. They are happy to be part of the team. They are not seeking to change the team into something they think it should be. They are not trying to move it from the strengths it has to the strengths they think it should have. You are looking for those who have a deep commitment to your congregation and to the mission of God.

There is no such thing as commitment in general. Oh, there may be in some people. Nevertheless, you are not looking for that kind of commitment. Some people may see themselves as "committed," but such generalized commitment is too vague to generate focused action. Indeed, sometimes it turns out that their sense of commitment is to whatever agenda they have. This does not help. What helps is their commitment to the specific mission, the team, and the congregation.

## Leadership Qualities

Look for the leadership qualities that people bring to the team. Look for the qualities in Set A and steer clear, as best you can, from those in Set B:

| Set A | Set B |
|---|---|
| Wisdom | Wanting to be boss |
| Proactivity | Managing |
| Shepherding | Enabling |
| Team thinking | Crisis mongering |

Many people have more than one of these leadership qualities. At the same time, some lead primarily with the gift of wisdom and discernment. You are helped by people who lead with wisdom rather than those who have a tendency to lead by trying to be the boss. Wanting to be boss simply sets up power and authority issues that most groups already have enough of; they do not need the mixed blessing of even more bossiness.

Some people lead with a proactive, intentional sense of direction, knowing how to develop concrete objectives. The congregation discovers and achieves solid objectives. You do not want people whose primary understanding of leadership is to be a manager, in the sense of developing many rules and regulations, policies and procedures, conditions and stipulations. People do not respond positively to that way of leading.

Some lead in more of a shepherding, supportive spirit. Their interest is in the person more than the process. You are not looking for the enabler who develops intricate processes of planning that take nearly forever to conclude. The process, unfortunately, becomes the plan. The journey takes too long. People get off the boat before anyone comes close to arriving at the destination.

Some lead with their capacity to develop a team. We are not looking for the person who sees leadership as being a charismatic inspirer. Those leaders deliver us into one apocalyptic crisis after another (sometimes it almost seems they fabricate them). Then they function as the savior of the day. People finally tire of the roller coaster of crises. They become immune. They lose interest. It becomes harder and harder to rev up for the new crisis. The team withers. Rather, we are looking for those with the leadership quality of knowing how to build a team. Many people have team ability (which we discuss next). Some people have the leadership quality of knowing how to *build* a team. They do so on the internal strengths and competencies of the team rather than on some external crisis that may, in the final analysis, serve more as a demotivator than a motivator.

Were you to have four people on a key leadership group, each of whom brings one of these leadership qualities—wisdom, proactivity, shepherding, and team thinking—you would have a solid team. Their gifts in leadership would stir comparable gifts in the congregation, and the number of constructive volunteers and leaders would grow.

## Team Ability

As you assess the gifts that people bring with them, look at their team ability. People tend to parallel their experiences. One clue to someone's capacity to function on a team is to look at the role she played in a recent, significant group in her life. The person who plays the role of team leader in one group tends to do the same in another group. The person who is an excellent team member in one group is likely to be the same in another group.

Someone who has been a maverick or rebel in one group tends to live out a similar role in another group, unless that role is already occupied by someone else. If so, the two either compete for the role or, in some instances, shift to another role with which they are familiar. The person who was a loner or a "ball hog" in a recent, significant group in his life tends to replicate the same role in another group.

A second clue to a person's capacity to function on a team is to look at the role he played in a prior, significant group in his life. It may be his original family, or a group in his school years, or one in his early work years. At the same time, we do grow and develop. The role he learned in an earlier group may no longer be where he is now.

A third clue to a person's team ability is her distance from her age-and-culture orientation. All of us are born into a specific age, and we develop a given cultural orientation. Those born in a certain cultural time learn a specific life question. In recent times, we can identify four age-cultural orientations. Indeed, these seem to have a recurring dynamic across much of human history. There may be other orientations, but these four seem to be persistently present.

People born into an age of pioneering learn the question, "Where are we headed?" This is a heading-out time. It is a time of confidence and assurance. It is a time of exploring and discovery. There are new vistas over the horizon. There are oceans to be sailed. There are plains and mountains to be crossed. There are stars to be explored. There are new possibilities to be discovered. The future looks strong and certain.

People born into an age of scarcity learn the question, "How much does it cost?" The lack of food, goods, and jobs makes what precious little we have important to our day-to-day survival. We eat what is on our plate because there is not that much on our plate. We do not want to waste what little we have.

People born into an age of affluence learn the question, "Which one shall we buy?" We cannot decide. We buy both. Food, goods, and jobs are plentiful. There is much food on our plate. We still try to clean our plate. We gain weight.

People born into an age of the future learn the question, "What is our future?" The question is asked with some doubt and uncertainty. Enough wars-to-end-all-wars have come and gone to cause us to have our doubts about a more promising future. Indeed, it is not clear that there will be a future, let alone that it will be constructive.

People with team ability have developed some distance on the age-cultural orientation they learned early on. The finance chair, born into an age of scarcity, does not automatically ask, "How much does it cost?" when the youth director, born into an age of affluence, wants to buy something. The finance chair has enough understanding of the influence that an age of scarcity had on his early life, and an age of affluence on the youth director's life, to listen thoughtfully to the proposal rather than react to it. The youth director too has enough understanding of these mutual influences to share the proposal in a thoughtful spirit.

These four cultural orientations are simultaneous and dynamic, not simply sequential and chronological. Some people, born in the depression of the 1930s, lived, during that time, in such lavishly affluent families that they learned a culture of affluence, not scarcity. Likewise, some people born in the 1960s were so desperately poor that, even during that prosperous time, they learned a culture of scarcity, not affluence.

What helps all of us as Christians is that we are a people reborn into an age of mission. As Christians, we learn the central question, "Who is our mission?" We ask the question with confidence and assurance. We know that God goes before us, leading us to the future that God is promising and preparing for us.

We know God gives us strengths sufficient to the mission to which God invites us. We know the future is in God's hands. We live in hope. In this spirit, our team ability is not of our own doing. It is the gift of God. The glue that binds us together as a team is the grace of God and the future to which God invites us.

## Integrity

Look for the integrity that people bring to the team. You are looking for people with a sense of honesty. They do not lie. They do not seek to cover up mistakes, nor do they take undue credit for success. They do not tell half-truths. They do not tell you only what you want to hear. They share the truth as best they can.

They have character. There is a soundness and sureness to their spirit. They do not play the mother-father game, wherein someone says no to what she wants to do but she then runs to someone else for a yes. They do not play people against one another. They know who they are. They have solid self-esteem, without being arrogant or egotistical.

Yes, they are sometimes anxious and fearful. However, they do not allow themselves to become frozen in fear and anxiety. Their spirit is proactive and intentional, not reactive and passive. They have a sense of values. They bring a sense of honor to their lives, and they stir a spirit of honor in those around them. They value the qualities that make life worthwhile.

## Growth

Look for people who are growing in the Christian life. I put this last, not because it is least important but because it is foundational with all of the others. It is as we are growing in our relationship with God that our competencies, our spirit of compassion, our commitment, our leadership qualities, our team ability, and our integrity advance and develop. All these are gifts from God. The more we discover the grace of these gifts, the more we grow the whole of who we are, and whose we are.

How we live shares the faith we have. I did not say, "growing in the Christian faith." Faith without life is dead. Faith is more than belief or talk. It is not that we have faith and then somehow talk faith. The talk is the walk. We are a living, breathing, walking theology.

How we live teaches people the faith we have. Faith lives in our lives as we behave in whole, healthy ways. We share our faith as we live our faith. Our faith is living testimony to the grace of God, the compassion of Christ, and the healing hope of the Holy Spirit. Look for people who are growing and developing, advancing and building whole, healthy lives in the grace of God.

Know where to look. Look in all seven groupings God gives you. Know what to look for. Look for the strengths that people bring with them. You will discover the team God is seeking to give you. As you do so, begin to think of growing your team.

# 10

# Growing
# Your Team

Ida Mae Stratton donated the land. Rudy Carl volunteered to serve as contractor. Plans were drawn. Various people contributed the brickwork, the plumbing, the electrical work, and the painting. It was a team effort. In the space of a few short months, the new parsonage was built. For the first time in its history, the congregation had a parsonage. This meant a community could now have a pastor living in the town.

We looked at the objective. We looked at the resources of the team. We drew a plan that matched what we could do. We moved forward. To be sure, in the early discussions of the project, there were many ideas as to the kind, the size, and the shape of the house to be built. We had wonderful discussions about the possibilities.

We matched the plan with the players. We built a house that matched our strengths, that we could do simply and soundly. The house is well built, precisely because we built a house we knew how to build. We moved forward with the spirit of being a team, a family, a congregation that had one clear objective—with a realistic and achievable time horizon. It worked. We celebrated well.

In the years come and gone, a number of pastors have blessed the community with their shepherding and preaching. The life of the community has been enriched. Children have been welcomed into the family, young people have discovered Christ, couples have been married, people have been visited in the hospital, parting funerals have been helpfully led, celebrations have been shared, people have discovered the grace of God. The spillover values have been extraordinary. The parsonage is serving well.

## Decide Your Objectives

You can build the team if you know the objectives. Some basketball teams run a fast break and full-court press. Some bring the ball down in a more methodical, steady manner. Some music groups play jazz. Some enjoy cantatas. Some football teams run a shotgun, short- and long-pass approach to the game. Some win, three and four yards on each running play. Some quilt groups make blocks and gather to put together a certain kind of quilt, in honor of the remarkable work of a leader. Or they make another kind of quilt to give to new babies in a nearby hospital, or yet another kind to share sympathy with a family on the loss of a loved one. There are many possible objectives, many different ways, to make quilts, sing music, or win games.

The way you plan shapes the objectives you decide and the team you grow. The art is to discover, with grassroots planning, the objectives that work well with your team. The more people involved in the planning, the more volunteers you have to achieve the plan. Congregational planning yields grassroots support to accomplish the plan.

In your first three months, lay the groundwork for a grassroots planning retreat to gather as many people in the congregation as possible. Together, as a congregation, you discover the future toward which God is inviting you. Were you to move to your new congregation in early July, then take July, August, and September to discover your team. In your shepherding, preaching, leading, and community presence, you are learning about your congregation and community. In the process, you are laying the groundwork for deciding the objectives that advance the health of your congregation. Then, you can have an excellent planning retreat, in October, November, or early December—your choice.

Before your retreat, encourage as many people as possible— grassroots members, Sunday school classes, women's groups, men's groups, the various committees, the church council, and the administrative board—to plan to be part of the retreat. Help all of them know you will have good fun and good times on the retreat. Invite them to be in prayer for the retreat. Help them look forward to the retreat as a time of discovery and moving forward.

On the retreat, have fun. Share good times. Help your congregation

- Claim its strengths
- Decide which one or two current strengths to expand
- Discover which one or two new strengths to add
- Create a simple action plan to advance your future

To expand a current strength, we are looking for two to four key objectives. To add a new strength, we are looking for four, or at most six, key objectives. With the retreat, we discover the few strengths and objectives that help us become an even stronger, healthier congregation. We discover the objectives we sense God inviting us to grow and develop for our future.

On your planning retreat, have a sense of your own priorities. The leader who knows her own priorities creates people who know their priorities. Share your priorities with a spirit of flexibility. The leader who is flexible creates people who are flexible. By contrast, the leader who insists on his own way creates people who insist on their own way. What you want is a planning retreat where we share a common search for what God is inviting us to achieve in mission. This grassroots, broadly based planning retreat helps us discover the way forward.

To help with their planning retreats, many congregations study the suggestions and principles in *Twelve Keys to an Effective Church* before they hold their retreat. However you resource your retreat, focus on your strengths. Do better what you do best. Build your strengths. Add new strengths. Look to the mission to which God is inviting you. You will have a wonderful retreat.

As a long-range planning committee, I encourage you *not* to select a small group of people to meet principally among themselves regularly for several months, or even a year or two. They will simply produce a lengthy plan that then sits on a shelf, as I suggested in Chapter Six. The difficulty with this approach to planning is that the small committee has ownership for their plan, but no one else in the congregation does. There is now a major problem. The committee members have to figure out how to sell their very detailed, highly-crafted, long-range planning report to the grassroots congregation. This is a top-down approach to planning.

With a new congregation, or in a new beginning with a current congregation, what helps you is a grassroots approach to planning. Gather as many people as possible in the congregation to participate in the planning retreat. Expand and add a few strengths. Discover a few key objectives. Grow forward your future.

Effective long-range planning looks more like a fast break down the basketball court than a neat, tidy ninety-seven-page plan. Do not to try to think of everything you plan to do in the coming three to five years. The art is to discover a few objectives you can accomplish and achieve now. Get moving with strong action and momentum. You will discover new objectives as you move forward.

We cannot steer a ship unless it is moving. Whether it be a sailboat or a power boat, when it sits dead in the water we cannot steer it in any direction. The naval term is that the ship is "in irons." When the ship is moving, we can steer it. We can make course corrections to a new direction. We can advance and improve our initial plan. But we need the initial plan to get moving in a healthy direction.

Thus, on your planning retreat, you discover your current strengths. You decide to expand one or more of them, and to add one or more new strengths. You find the few key objectives that grow and develop the mission of your congregation. For your immediate future, select one current strength to expand and one new strength to add. Move forward on the few key objectives to achieve each.

You will have a streamlined plan with strong ownership by the grassroots members of the congregation. You avoid the temptation, in the enthusiasm of your new beginning, of seeking to put in place too many goals that sound too busy and too hurried. You illustrate with your people—as a wise, caring leader—that you have the discernment to know what really counts, what is really important, what really matters in helping people with their lives and destinies.

Because you include a number of others in the planning, you achieve these objectives with the help of many people in your congregation. When you accomplish them, be graceful. Be easy to live with. Do not blow your own horn, toot your own whistle, prance and parade for what *you* have done. A team of people has succeeded with your leadership and with theirs. Give gratitude to God and give thanks to your congregation.

# Structure Your Team

Form follows function. Structure follows strategy. Organization follows objectives. Once you know your players and decide your objectives, you can structure your team. There is no point in convening committees simply because they are on some organizational chart somewhere. The art is to save the structure until you know where you are heading. Then, structure the teams that lead you forward.

## Teams

In our time, people are searching for community, not committee. They are searching for action, not analysis. *A team is a group of people who actively accomplish some objective.* They do just enough analysis that they know where they are heading. They invest most of their time and energy in the action and less in meetings. People are happy to be part of such a group and to have a sense of satisfaction that in the end they achieve their objective. They are glad to be part of a team.

People are less interested in being on a committee. It is the case in many committees that the focus is practically on meeting for the sake of meeting. This is not true of all committees, but it is the case that many committee members invest more time and energy in the meetings and less in the action. To be sure, some good decisions are made. Some useful work is achieved. Nevertheless, the emphasis is on meeting monthly or weekly to discuss what they might do at some point in the future. People do not gain enough of a sense of satisfaction and accomplishment out of such a group to believe that participating in one is worthwhile.

People are drawn to a team that has a specific mission. They are less drawn to a committee whose preoccupation is institutional. They look forward to participating on a team whose compelling focus is mission, not organization, whose emphasis is on service, not survival. They want to be directly involved in helping people with their lives and destinies.

People are drawn to a team that is invitational, not institutional. That is, the spirit of the group is open, inclusive, warm, and welcoming. The group has an inviting spirit, encouraging new members and new ideas. People are less interested in a group that simply has an institutional concern for perpetuating the group. People are more generous than that. People want their lives to count for more than that. They like being a part of a team that is making a genuine difference in the health and vitality of the wider community.

## Team Possibilities

You can structure five kinds of teams:

1. One-time

2. Seasonal

3. Short-term

4. Long-term

5. Weekly or monthly year-round

I encourage you to have many one-time, seasonal, and short-term teams. Both excellent sprinters and solid marathon runners will participate. You may have a few long-term and weekly or monthly teams, but I hope you put your organizational emphasis on the first three possibilities.

Habitat for Humanity is built on the premise of one-time teams. The emphasis is "Come, one time, and build one house." I know many people who have built several houses, but they were not asked to build a house a year. They were asked to build a specific house. Then they were asked to build another house.

Growing out of your congregational planning retreat, several specific objectives are what I think of as one-timers. Each can be given to a one-time team that has the fun and satisfaction of accomplishing the specific objective. Some objectives can be given to a seasonal team. An objective related to vacation Bible school, which occurs seasonally, can be given to a seasonal team.

Some teams function in a short-term, highly intensive manner. In three to five sessions, whether over three to five weeks or three to five months, they achieve their objective. The objective might be an Advent Bible study of three sessions, or it could be a Lenten Bible study of five sessions. By definition, short-term teams focus on three to five sessions.

By contrast, long-term teams focus on six or more sessions to achieve their objective. Weekly or monthly year-round teams focus on their objective regularly and routinely throughout the whole year. Solid marathon runners thrive on these two kinds of teams. Excellent sprinters die.

Regrettably, most organizational structures are designed by solid marathon runners. Usually, a committee is established to develop the structure. There is a high density of solid marathon runners on the committee. It takes being a marathon runner to serve on the committee. To do its work, the committee meets in a marathon-runner manner. It is not surprising that what they design is a marathon-runner structure.

Following your congregational planning retreat, or as part of it, have a one-time structure session to create the one-time, seasonal, short-term, long-term, weekly, and monthly teams to accomplish the objectives. Do not simply assign the emerging objectives to your "standing committees." But if you do, teach them how to set up one-time, seasonal, and short-term teams to achieve many of the objectives.

If you assign all of the objectives to standing committees, they may sit on them. That is, they may seek to achieve them slowly, steadily, and routinely. Some objectives are appropriately accomplished this way. However, many objectives can be achieved by one-time, seasonal, and short-term teams. Develop much of your structure in this way.

## Team Descriptions

In our time, we need to help structure each team with a simple, streamlined *team description*. (The earlier term was *job description,* but I see a team description as fundamentally different from the job descriptions of an earlier time.) Each team leader, by extension, helps each person on the team have a comparable team description for his or her action and accomplishment. The team description, whether for the team or for each person, is mutually developed and has several components:

*Two to four key objectives.* The objectives that the person counts on achieving connect directly to the strengths your congregation has decided to expand and add in its congregational planning retreat. These objectives are specific and concrete, realistic and achievable, and they have solid time horizons. When a team or person has more than four key objectives, it is too many. It is usually a setup to fail. With two to four, we can succeed.

*Four major responsibilities central to the key objectives.* Both the team and each person on the team may fulfill other responsibilities during the course of the year. What is helpful is that they both know and fulfill the four primary responsibilities connected directly to their two to four key objectives. A long list of eight to fifteen responsibilities is not a job description. It is a merry-go-round of activities that goes nowhere but around and around.

*One growth objective.* Each person selects a competency she looks forward to growing in herself during the year. The team, as a whole, does likewise.

*The team's (and team member's) authority.* The more authority you help people discover, the healthier the team and the congregation become. Authority comes in three ways: leadership, decisions, and budget. The more authority people have, the more likely they are to grow, and the more ownership they have for their objectives.

*Straight-line accountability.* Multiple lines of accountability do not create solid teams. They contribute to confused teams. If you want the person who is the team leader to be the leader, talk to him or her. By letting your enthusiasm and easy-going nature bring you to bypass the leader and talk directly to members of the team, you undermine the leader, even if unintentionally.

A team description having these five components advances the effectiveness of your teams and of each person on them.

Some congregations develop detailed, elaborate job descriptions that include many major and minor responsibilities. Compulsion toward perfectionism is at work there. The team description previously given focuses on the major objectives that deliver most of the results for the year. Each team knows where it is heading and sees the connection between its objectives and the grassroots plan that emerged from the congregational planning retreat.

Therefore, all your teams are heading in a common direction, building the whole of your future, rather than being preoccupied with the parts. The art is to focus on the whole more than the parts. In an earlier time, committees and volunteers were given long lists of responsibilities to perform. The focus was on the parts. This caused many congregations to have a departmental approach. People became concerned with their own area and lost sight of the whole. But if we know our grassroots congregational plan and the key objectives each team contributes to achieving the plan, we can move forward in a whole, healthy spirit.

# Coach Your Team

You coach your team with listening, encouragement, positive reinforcement, and coaching evaluation.

## Listening

You coach your team forward more by listening than by telling. When you invest your time in telling, they may in fact do what you tell them to do. However, their ownership of what they do is minimal. Further, they come to depend on your telling them before they do anything. Reactively and passively, they wait on your instructions. If you listen, you create people who are proactive and intentional and internalize the objectives they plan to achieve. You create people with initiative and ingenuity.

The person who listens is listened to. The person who does not listen is not listened to. If you listen, wisely and well, you create people who listen more fully to you and to those around them. If you do not listen to them, you create people who do not listen to you; nor do they listen to those around them. People lead in the way you lead them.

The more you listen to their excellent ideas and good suggestions, the more they own both your leadership and what they do. Further, people listen in the way they are listened to. In your listening, you teach them to listen to the people with whom they are working. As you listen, you learn the art of listening and teach people the art of listening.

The more you listen, the more you learn. Frequently, the best ideas come from those closest to the action. Their creativity and inventiveness are nurtured as you listen to them. You can listen at three levels: to what is said, to what is between the lines, and to what is not said. Frequently, you learn as much by what is not said as by what is said.

## Encouragement

During the time the team members are working on an objective, you coach them forward more by encouraging than by scolding. Have more interest in them than in what they can do for you. You can learn while you teach people the grace of encouragement. You can help people, amid their anxiety and their fears, their anger and their rages, to discover some positive growth and development, some sense of advancing and building their own lives.

Many pastors serve healthy congregations. Some pastors, however, do not know what to do with a healthy congregation, so they make it unhealthy; then they know what to do. These pastors hold the notion that congregations have problems and they themselves have the solutions. They think congregations have questions and they themselves have the answers.

In point of fact, many congregations do pretty well. Oh, they have their share of difficulties and problems, but overall they are healthy and strong. What they benefit from is some encouragement for what they are doing. What they long for is someone with integrity who has learned the art of encouraging them in a constructive spirit.

When things are not going well, it is appropriate to say so, with honesty and integrity. People who learn the gift of encouragement do not gloss over difficulties. They call a spade a spade. They do not have a naïve, Pollyanna, superficial optimism. By the same token, they do not become preoccupied with the problems. They help the team discover a way forward.

## Positive Reinforcement

As your team is completing a key objective, you coach the members forward more by positive reinforcement than by negative reinforcement. Once they finish a key objective successfully, you deliver three things quickly and generously.

First, you say, "Well done." With integrity and generosity, you say thank-you. It amazes me that vast numbers of people know how to do this well but many pastors and leaders are still learning the art. The more you say "well done," the stronger the team becomes.

Second, you deliver new leadership. You do this by helping the team discover new possibilities with a broader base of leadership and a fuller range of authority. The two go together. What does not help is to give a team more to say grace over without also helping them claim the authority that goes with their new range of leadership. A key statement is found in the parable of the talents (Matthew 25:14–30): "Well done, good and faithful servant; you have been faithful over a few things; I will make thee *ruler* over many things [*set* you over much—R.S.V.; put you in *charge* of something big—N.E.B.]; enter into the joy of the Lord" (Matthew 25:21 and 23 K.J.V.).

The Lord gives more authority. The church frequently gives more responsibility without the commensurate authority. The more authority you help people claim, the more fully they have ownership for their new leadership possibilities.

Third, you reward them with recognition. The team does not achieve its objectives to gain recognition. Most teams accomplish their objectives for the sake of helping people with their lives and having the fun and satisfaction of doing so. Nevertheless, it is important for you to recognize their achievement. With volunteers, you can share generous recognition for their accomplishment, in some public manner or privately.

With staff, you can do the same. Also, with staff you can share a bonus or merit increase in salary, or provide some other tangible benefit in compensation. It could take the form of days off, vacation time, pension contribution, or whatever. The more generous you are, the more likely they are to be generous with their growth and future achievements.

## Coaching Evaluation

You coach your team forward by helping the members develop their capacity for evaluation. The pro, in any field, is the person who has an "onboard" capacity for self-evaluation. During an operation, we want a pro surgeon who has this capacity. The amateur is one who has not yet developed it.

Put it this way. You can deliver listening, encouragement, and positive reinforcement to grow your team. All of these things are supportive if you also have a constructive approach to evaluation. However, they are all undone by a less-than-helpful approach to evaluation.

To be sure, there are several approaches to evaluation. One is what I call an "other" approach. In this approach, some other individual or group evaluates the person. The difficulties in this approach cause some groups to have "no" approach to evaluation. They simply do not evaluate. The negatives of the "other" approach are so manifest that the latter groups simply avoid any form of evaluation. Minus any positive process of evaluation, people do not grow.

In some groups without an evaluation process, what emerges is "grapevine" evaluation. This inevitably leads to gossip, innuendo, and rumor. Tattle and hearsay comments do not help people grow. In some groups, the evaluation process is built on "petty" and "picky." The process is not substantive. It does not focus on the key areas for the team or the person's growth. It nitpicks around the edges. Regrettably, the more that petty and picky show up, the more likely that "pity" is not far behind. People do not grow when pity comes their way.

How you evaluate is decisive in growing the team. You do not grow your team by doing an evaluation of their work. With volunteers and staff, the old notion was that their superior, at the end of the year, would do a performance review and evaluation of the person's work for the year. This top-down, "other" evaluation process creates passive-aggressive behavior, low-grade hostility, subliminal resentment, and eruptive forms of anger.

The most tragic result of such a process is none of these. The most tragic result is the person loses the capacity for self-evaluation. In the "other" approach to evaluation, someone else evaluates the person. The way people learn self-evaluation is by doing self-evaluation. In *Effective Church Leadership*, you will discover two chapters that help you with the specifics of how to develop coaching, consultive evaluation for yourself, your staff, and your volunteers.

For our purposes here, I simply want to confirm that how you, your volunteers, and your staff develop the capacity for self-evaluation is decisive in growing the team. In AA and Al-Anon, the person in recovery is invited to develop his or her capacity for self-evaluation. With the help of a sponsor and a twelve-step program, they are encouraged to grow themselves forward.

I encourage you to develop your capacity for self-evaluation and to help your team do likewise. Indeed, one of the best ways to coach your team is to develop your own capacity for self-evaluation. It is harder to help others grow if you do not plan to grow yourself. You help others grow as you grow yourself.

Discover your team. Decide your objectives. Structure your team. Coach your team. Do these things with the spirit in which God invites us to new life, to discover a more abundant life in the grace of God. Let the growing of your team have this spirit of discovery and grace.

# 11

# Developing
# Your Future

Gene died in a boating accident. It happened on a day
when the lake was hardly being used. There were so few
boats out. People still cannot quite figure out how it happened. It was not his fault, but he is, nonetheless, dead. His
wisdom and humor are greatly missed. The family and the
congregation grieved for a long time.

Harriet is raising her three grandchildren. This was a sud-
den development in her life. Her daughter and son-in-law
divorced. More accurately, one day he up and deserted the
family. After a period of time in which the family kept hoping
he would come back, her daughter filed for and was granted
a divorce.

Harriet's daughter has returned to college. What with her
daughter going to school full-time and working full-time, the
net result is that Harriet is raising her three grandchildren. In
the early days, her bones creaked a lot and she discovered
muscles in her body she had forgotten were still there.

It has been two years and she has hit her stride. Each morning with the kids is a new adventure. There have been some
tough times. Her oldest grandchild was especially troubled

by the departure of her dad. It took her a long time to get over her dad's leaving.

The oldest is now in junior high, but fortunately the younger two go to the same elementary school. For Harriet, it makes carpooling easier. They are all active in the church. The kids sing in the children's and youth choirs. Harriet and all three of the children have discovered a rhythm of life that works well for all of them.

Most days they have fun together. Harriet is teaching her granddaughter how to make grape pies. They are turning out good. The family recipe is being passed to the next generation.

Janet is now the vice president of the bank. She has a gift for working well with people. She has the ability to assess good loan prospects for new businesses. She is the most respected vice president the community has known. When the congregation needed a loan to help construct the new youth building, Janet worked out a very favorable arrangement for the church.

There is talk that when Mr. Roberts retires as president in a couple of years, the board will name Janet as the new president. She would be the first woman president of a bank in the community.

For several years, Janet served as leader of the finance team for the congregation. She was recently put on the board of trustees of the church. This was unusual since she and her family are not really old-timers in the church. Her wisdom is greatly respected.

Ben has softened in the years that have come and gone. He listens better. He is less quick to say whatever comes to his mind. He is more at peace with himself. When his stepfather died, he was greatly moved by the compassion his pastor shared with him. A year later, when his mother followed, the quiet shepherding of his pastor helped him through her death.

He was appreciative that his pastor remembered him the first Christmas after each of their deaths.

Ben's choir, everyone says, has gotten better. They seem happier with one another. They are more like a family. The music is more stirring and inspiring. Rehearsals are more fun. Several new people have joined, and their spirit has helped. People say Ben has come into his own.

Sue continues to teach history. She has become the legendary teacher of the school. From time to time, her graduates look her up to thank her for the spirit of learning they discovered with her. She receives cards at Christmas and notes at the time of college graduations.

Several of her students have gone on to do master's degrees in history, looking to the time when they will teach. She can see that the children of some of her early students will soon be in her classes. She agreed to serve, several years ago, as leader of the personnel team for the congregation. People genuinely appreciate her leadership with the team.

From time to time, Sue instigates a gathering of herself, Harriet, Janet, and Ben for fun and fellowship. They miss Gene's oatmeal cookies, but the grape pie, the orange and grapefruit slices, the coffee, and the lemon pie are sufficient for their time together. Occasionally, Sue brings a cherry pie in place of her lemon pie.

Most of the time, unless he is tied up at the hospital or leading an event with youth in the community, Marvin joins with them. The second or third time they got together, Sue invited him. He does not take Gene's place. No one could. He has his own place. He has been their pastor through all of the events, good and bad, hopeful and tragic, that have come and gone.

On the occasion of their fifth or sixth gathering—no one quite remembers which—Sue invited a new person, Betty, to come. It seemed natural. Betty became part of the congregation a few years before when she moved to the community as the result of a job transfer. Her company wanted her to be in the regional office. On a Sunday, she came to church. Almost by accident, she and Sue met. They were both coming in the front door of the church at the same time. They had a good conversation together.

Betty began to help with the vacation Bible school. She has a natural gift with children. Over time, she has become the leader of the school. With her leadership, the congregation now sees the vacation Bible school as their gift to the whole community. Children of the congregation, many of their friends, and hosts of children in the community come. It has become a major event for the whole community. It just seemed natural to Sue to include Betty in the gatherings.

Some time passed, and along the way Sue invited Jim to come. Jim coaches the church softball team in the summer. He has been doing it for several years. Way back, the church had a team. Then, for many years, there was no team.

Jim moved to town because he liked the area. He now runs the local hardware store. He started out as a clerk, then moved to the cash register, and then became manager. He and the owner have an agreement that when the owner retires in a few years, Jim will buy him out. Jim is already a part owner, and he has done much to help the store succeed.

Jim met Sally in the hardware store. She came to buy something. He helped her, and, a few weeks later, he invited her out. One thing led to another and they fell in love and decided to get married. Since neither of them had a church, and Jim knew Sue because she was a regular customer, he asked if they could be married in Sue's church. Sue put them in touch with the pastor. Marvin and Jim hit it off well. The wedding was wonderful. They began to attend worship.

A couple more years passed. They lost their first child in a miscarriage. Their second child was stillborn. They adopted a child. Two years after that, Sally gave birth to a healthy baby. A third child was born three years after that. Through all of the ups and downs, difficulties and celebrations, their pastor was with them. Sue encouraged Harriet and Janet to be supportive in those hard times. Ben took a liking to Jim and helped him through some of the tough times. Their pastor was gracious and kind, supportive and shepherding.

Somewhere along the way, Marvin proposed that he and Jim start a softball team for the youth of the community. Jim's own grief over the loss of their first two children was such that he turned the pastor down. A week or two later, Marvin showed up in the hardware store with a softball jersey with Jim's name on it. Gently, he said that the first practice would be Wednesday night. He said something like, "I think the team will be good for you, but whether it is or not, I know you will be good for the team."

The two of them had a wonderful season coaching the team. The next year, Jim was encouraged to become the lead coach of the team. He was a natural. The kids loved him. The church softball team became the best thing for youths in the community. Even more than before, Jim was respected for his leadership and abilities with young people. To Sue, it was natural to include Jim in their occasional gatherings.

When the Welcome Team gets together, Harriet brings her wonderful grape pie. Janet continues to bring her dish of orange and grapefruit slices, occasionally adding some other fruit. Ben brings his special coffees. He used to bring tea as well, but Betty now brings the herbal and regular teas. Sue brings her remarkable lemon pie. Learning that Gene used to bring oatmeal cookies, and having a recipe passed down in the family, Jim contributes the oatmeal cookies.

They have a feast of fun, food, and fellowship. Gene is there in spirit. Harriet, Janet, Ben, and Sue sense his presence. They are glad Betty and Jim have come on board. They add new wisdom and experience. Their pastor is with them as often as he can be. What started out as a Welcome Team has become a family—with Betty and Jim adding a richness and depth to their gatherings. They do not meet often, but when they do, it is like a warm, fun, family reunion.

The congregation has had good years since Marvin came as pastor. Some new members have joined. Mostly, the congregation is excited about its communitywide vacation Bible school and its softball team for the kids of the community. These activities have encouraged the congregation to gradually develop preschool, after-school, and summer programs for children and youths. The number of constituents and persons served in mission has markedly increased. A new worship service has been started that is serving many of them.

Their pastor is grateful for the new beginning with which the Welcome Team helped him so much. More than Marvin would have ever imagined, he has become a good shepherd, a helpful preacher, a wise leader, and a community pastor. He continues to be quietly amazed at how his ministry with the whole community has grown. He loves his congregation and they love him. He is glad to get together with Harriet, Janet, Ben, Sue, Betty, and Jim. They are part of his life, and he is part of theirs.

## Build on Mission

You develop your future as you build on your mission. Keep before you four missional, invitational questions. I call these invitational questions because they are the questions to keep ever before you. They are not questions to be answered, on the front end, with precision and finality. They are banner questions that go before you and lead you in a helpful missional direction—the kind of questions we ask to shape the future we are heading toward.

The first invitational question is, "Who is our mission?" That is, who is God inviting us to serve in mission? The question is people-centered, person-centered. The question leads us to our compassion and generosity, our passion and our purpose, our selflessness and our serving.

The question confirms that our central task is mission: helping people with their lives and destinies with the grace of God. I encourage you to stay away from the question "How can we get more members?" The way forward, particularly if yours is a weakened congregation, is to rediscover the missional purpose to which God invites you.

Frequently, God has planted our mission right in front of us. As we look with missional eyes, we see it and move to serve it. We live with the confidence that God will supply resources sufficient unto the mission we share. The stronger the mission, the richer the resources God gives us to advance the mission.

The question of how to get more members is, unfortunately, built on the premise that "we" need more members to do something. However, the mission does not depend on the resources "we alone" can muster. The mission depends on the resources that God provides. Indeed, most healthy missions live in continuing gratefulness for the resources that God is supplying. One way this happens is that we frequently discover new leaders to help with the mission from among the people who are helped in the mission.

The second invitational question is, "What are our strengths, gifts, and competencies?" The question affirms that we are given by God specific competencies and strengths to be a whole, healthy congregation. To be sure, there is a diversity of gifts. Some congregations have strengths in certain areas. Some have competencies in other areas.

I encourage you, especially in this time of a new beginning, not to pose the question "What do you see as the problems and concerns of the church?" This question distracts you and your congregation both from discovering your mission and from claiming your strengths. It distracts you from claiming your personal strengths. It reinforces any low self-esteem present in you or your congregation. You are welcome to get to the problems in due course.

People who deny their strengths deny God, deny God's gifts. Some people, and some congregations, suffer from low self-esteem, look down on themselves, and think more poorly of themselves than they have a right to do. They deny God and God's gifts.

It is more fun to have a new beginning *with* God than without God. When you begin with your strengths, gifts, and competencies, you begin with God; you begin with God's gifts. To be sure, you will want to adapt—that is, to bridge— your gifts to the mission field with which God blesses you. Strength and vitality have more merit than becoming larger or smaller.

The third invitational question is, "What kind of future are we building?" That is, what future are we developing for our families, our community, our world, and our congregation? I have listed these in their proper order. Do not put the church first in the order.

The question, as stated, invites us to focus beyond the institutional welfare or survival of our church. The question encourages us to build a team whose primary concerns are our families, community, and world. The focus is on mission, not institution. The focus is external and in the world, not internal and in the church. The question helps people think through the kind of future they are in fact building for their family, their community, and their world.

The question "What are the needs of our church?" is an institutional question. This question, and others like it, simply teaches the congregation that you are more interested in the church than you are in them. You teach them you have a functional, organizational, institutional perspective, and that you have come here to pastor the church as an institution rather than pastor the congregation as people who lead a healthy mission.

I encourage you not to ask, "If you could have three wishes for your church, what would they be?" Again, the focus is on the church. The preoccupation of the question is with the church. Sometimes, your people—both key leaders and grassroots members—want to talk at length about the church. You can focus the conversation by saying in invitation, "Share one or two excellent ideas, good suggestions we could have fun doing together in the coming three to five years." The focus is on one or two ideas, not ten or twenty. The focus is on good ideas, excellent suggestions, not on gossip and problems.

Given half a chance, people present excellent suggestions. The focus is on what "we could have fun doing together," not on what we should do or must do. The focus is on the coming three to five years, not this year only. The focus is on the future. Sometimes we build forward a winning team in three to five years.

The focus is on "we." The focus is collective, not singular. We are in this together. One way I say it is, "The team plays well for the coach that loves the team." The coach loves the team whether they win or lose. The coach does not love the team so they will win. The love is not a means to an end. The love is a gift, freely given.

The fourth invitational question is, "Where are we headed?" This question confirms we have a future we can head toward. This question confirms that we can head toward the future God is preparing for us. We do not live in the past. We look to the future, knowing God goes before us and leads us. God does not live in the past. God has acted graciously and mercifully, generously and hopefully in the past, and God has moved on to the present and the future.

The question "Where have we been?" has a focus on the past. From time to time, it may be a useful question. But it often invokes gossip about your predecessors, whether good or bad. You are not seeking to gossip, nor to hear gossip about various pastors or members. Leave your gossip-curiosity at home when you are with your people. You are not there to find out the history of your church. That, by itself, is still a focus on the church. If you have an interest in history, invite your people to share with you, as individuals, *their* history, and their hopes.

In a given visit or gathering, the conversation may move to the church. The subject may be brought up by the person you are visiting, either because this is an interest she has or because she has learned this is what ministers like to talk about. Should this happen, you might respond with this invitation: "Share with me about your life." You are keeping the conversation personal. The focus is still with the other person.

You are interested in the individual, not in the history of your predecessors, or in gossip about other church members, or in a recounting of all the conflicts that have happened in past years. All of these matters will come to you soon enough, if any are present. Keep the focus with the person.

Invite people to share something of where they were born and what has happened since. Encourage your people to share something of their *own* life's pilgrimage. In doing so, they will share with you both about their own history and the history of the congregation. If you state your question by asking about the church's history, that is all you will learn. If you focus on their history, you learn both. Visit with people about their past, their interests, their strengths, and their hopes for their life and future.

Listen for any grieving they may be doing over a beloved pastor who has just retired. Listen for celebratory events of good fun and good times. Listen for tragic events that may have scared and scarred people. Listen for a spirit that reveals we are strong and growing stronger.

Someone may say to you, "If people were only more committed and could see the challenge, our church would be doing better." Do not bite. This statement is not the focus of a new beginning. This is not how you develop your future. Keep your focus with the person, not the church. The grassroots members of a congregation motivate themselves on compassion and community, not challenge or commitment. These last two are the motivations present among some key leaders. The person you are focusing on may be teaching you he is a key leader, and that commitment and challenge are his primary motivations.

If these motivations were going to work with the grass roots, they would have worked by now. If you allow yourself to be drawn into a focus on commitment and challenge, you simply teach the grassroots congregation that your primary focus is with key leaders. People at the grass roots are drawn to a sense of compassion and a spirit of community. This is how they head to the future. In advancing your future, keep these invitational questions before you. Build on mission.

## Build on Health

You develop your future as you build on health. In a new beginning, begin with your best strengths. Begin with God's gifts. Whatever your best strengths are, they are the gifts of God. People who claim their strengths claim God, claim God's gifts. Wise, caring leaders build on sources of health and wholeness present in the congregation. In this regard, you will find *Twelve Keys for an Effective Church* helpful. You will find *Twelve Keys for Living: Possibilities for a Whole, Healthy Life* equally helpful. These two books are good friends, close companions. They help one another.

Healthy congregations create healthy people. It is equally true that healthy people create healthy congregations. You have a twofold focus: to help your congregation be strong and healthy, and to help people in your congregation lead strong, healthy lives. The two go together.

*For the most part, you will discover you are serving a healthy congregation.*

I have written this phrase in italics so you will grasp that most congregations are strong and healthy. There are, in fact, three kinds of congregations: strong and healthy, weak and declining, and dying.

Focus on strength and health rather than size. Develop with your congregation a future that is strong and healthy.

A regrettable emphasis on size comes from the misbegotten notion that only large congregations will thrive in the years to come. In *Building for Effective Mission,* I discuss four futures for congregations in the twenty-first century:

1. Mega
2. Large, regional
3. Middle
4. Small and strong

For most congregations, one of the last three—large and regional, healthy and midsized, or small and strong—is their best future.

It is not true that bigger is better. Bigger is simply bigger, not necessarily better. We have romanticized bigness too much. To counter that, some people also romanticize smallness: "Thank God we are small and are getting smaller."

Many megacongregations are strong and healthy. Some megacongregations are in trouble. They are weak and declining. Likewise, many large, regional congregations are strong and healthy. Some are declining. Some are dying. The same is true for small congregations. Not all small congregations are declining and dying. Many are strong and healthy. The key is to focus on strength more than size. You will discover you are serving a healthy congregation. The vast majority of congregations are strong and healthy.

Still, you might discover you are serving a weak, declining congregation or a dying one. Most declining or dying congregations do not become so because people are lazy, apathetic, or indifferent. They decline or die because a small group of people—deeply committed, highly challenged—are working very hard on the wrong things. They are working on the things that worked in the 1940s and 1950s but do not work in the 1990s and beyond the year 2000.

Frequently, declining or dying congregations become preoccupied with the sources of illness more than the sources of health. They become problem-based. They focus on their problems, needs, concerns, weaknesses, and shortcomings. Now, they are not accidentally problem-based. They learned this behavior pattern somewhere. Sometimes, it is learned from ministers who have a problem-based approach to life and church. Sometimes, people bring this approach to their church because it is the approach to life they have learned in their everyday life.

When you find this problem-based approach to life, the key is to help people discover sources for health and wholeness. The key is to help them learn a health-based approach to life. Otherwise, you help them solve the current presenting problem. You mistakenly think that once this problem is solved, then you can move on to develop your future.

The catch is that a problem-based approach simply finds a new problem for you to solve. In a way, the approach is "Our problem is _____ (fill in the blank)." The real problem is not the presenting problem, which changes swiftly. The real problem is the underlying approach to life that looks at life with a problem-based mentality.

With a problem-based congregation, the art is to help members find one strength they have. Focus on how you can expand this one strength. This can often be done through several (one to three) one-time events. Once you expand a current strength, then you can look to add one new strength. Add it through several (one to three) one-time events. Build on the sources of health God gives you.

I want you to remember that the vast majority of congregations are strong and healthy. Otherwise, they would not exist as long as they do. To be sure, congregations that are declining or dying are highly resilient. It takes a long time for a congregation to die. I have worked with dying churches where some alleged expert had been there twenty-five years earlier, saying, "If you don't do such and such, you're going to die." Twenty-five years come and go and the church is still there.

People do not move forward in response to threats. I have never yet met a single person wrestling with alcoholism who gave up drinking because someone said, "If you don't give up your drinking, you're going to die." Saying so simply intensifies the problem, accentuates the anxiety, increases the difficulty, and advances the drinking.

Declining and dying congregations last a long time. Moreover, they do not respond to threat. Indeed, they become almost immune to that ploy, since they have seen it so many times. Your best possibility is to build on whatever strength, however fragile and feeble, is present in the congregation. Build on health.

Indeed, you are there to build on health and wholeness no matter whether the congregation is strong, weak, or dying. Look for the sources of health. In medicine, in years past, the focus was primarily on the illness. This is an important focus. In medicine, more recently, it is on the sources of health and hope. Train your selective perception to look for the strengths. Build on these. God will help grow forward this congregation.

You will want to spend more time building on the central characteristics that are the sources of health and wholeness in your congregation than on the problems. Do not rush to find the weaknesses. If you find the strengths first, you are in the strongest position to tackle the weaknesses. When you begin with the weaknesses, you are in the weakest position to tackle them. Claim the strengths. Build on those strengths. Do better what you do best. Build on health.

## Build on Hope

Teach your congregation that you are hopeful. Oh, I do not mean that you are hopeful about the future of the church. That is an entirely different matter. How quickly we reduce the richness of hope to whether a given church is going to survive, let alone thrive.

Teach your congregation that you are hopeful about life. Help them learn that you are a growing and developing person, that you are flexible, that you are not caught in the ways in which you have always done things, that you look forward to learning new possibilities. Help them discover that you live in hope, not because it is of your own doing but because it is the gift of God. You live with the confidence and assurance that the source of your hope comes from God. It is not that you are pulling yourself up by your spiritual bootstraps. It is not that the origin of your hope is in you. Hope comes from God.

Life has its share of twists and turns, calamities and difficulties. We wrestle with temptation. We struggle with sin. Terrible tragedies come to us. Death awaits us. There are good times, times of rejoicing and celebration. The sad times and the happy times seem to come now here, now there. We lose friends and family, and God sends us new friends to be family with us. We are wise enough to know God gives us the hope and capacity to deal with all that life brings us. We are not in this life alone. God is with us, surrounding us with grace and hope.

To be sure, we discover enough despair, depression, and despondency in life that we sometimes lose heart. The times when we are most panicked, most anxious, most angry are lost to history (though too quickly called to mind). We cling to the times of confidence and assurance, the times when we are healthy and hopeful. We experience times of credibility and integrity, trust and respect. We long for more such times.

We seek to advance, well and wisely, the hope God gives us. We do not want to spend it foolishly, lavishly. Likewise, we do not want to bury it in the ground, hoping we can conserve and hold, protect and preserve it. The more we give hope away, the more hope grows in us.

Teach people that you are hopeful. Illustrate your sense of hope by the way you live your life. Demonstrate your hope by the way you grow yourself forward, with the hope of God. In your new beginning, live as a flexible, learning, growing person. Share the gifts of grace, encouragement, and hope with yourself as well as your congregation.

Some pastors seek to share these gifts with their congregation but do not share them with themselves. When you share them with yourself, you are in a healthier position to share them with your congregation. When you share the gift of hope with yourself, you find a sense of peace and discovery.

In a new beginning, you are in a healthy position to discover the new possibilities to which God invites you. Among the following possibilities, choose the ones that help you grow in yourself a richer, fuller spirit of hope:

- Claim one gift and competency you have so as to be more fully a good shepherd, a helpful preacher, a wise and caring leader, and a community pastor.
- Discover one new insight about your life that encourages you.
- Participate in one mission outreach—in a one-time event—in your community to which you sense God is inviting you now.
- Decide on one action objective you plan to achieve that will permit you to advance the health of your congregation early on.
- Choose one growth objective in your own strengths, gifts, and competencies that you plan early on to grow and develop in yourself.
- Decide on one activity or behavior pattern that you plan to quit now.
- Discover one source of hope that is important to you.

Of these seven possibilities, select three or four that advance your own growth and your own sense of hope. In so doing, you encourage your people to a richer, fuller sense of hope in their own lives. This renewed spirit of hope spills over into your congregation.

I encourage you to build this spirit of hope in your own life and in the lives of your people. Begin with life; then move to church. So often, we begin with church. But, when people are struggling to find hope in life, it is even more difficult for them to have hope for their congregation. When they find the hope of God in their lives, they more easily have hope for their congregation.

It would be a travesty to try to help people have hope for their congregation and to achieve the objective only to ignore helping them discover sources of hope for their own lives. This would be a most self-centered project. God loves the world. God has hope for the world. It is not that God just loves the church. It is not that God just has hope for the church.

People live on hope. God invites us to help them discover hope for their lives. It is a larger, more profound task than simply helping them find hope for their church. Help people discover the richness of hope, and they live lives of grace, encouragement, peace, and hope.

We are drawn to hope because of the integrity with which hope helps us with our lives. As we experience the hope of God, powerfully, quietly, remarkably, our lives become whole. We live with a sense that life is stirring and inspiring. We discover grace and power, compassion, and joy.

The hope we discover may focus on a specific human hurt, such as grieving the loss of a loved one, wrestling with some form of addiction, or searching for ways to live whole and healthy lives. It may focus on a life stage such as the move from preschool to first grade, the move from elementary school to junior high, the move to a marriage, a first child, or a first grandchild. It may focus on a community interest or concern, such as education, safety, family, or volunteerism.

In the first three months, whether in a new congregation or with a new beginning in a present congregation, build what you do on the hope with which God blesses you. As you develop your plans for these three months, focus first on your hope for living a whole, healthy life. You are in the strongest position to help your congregation with their lives if you are developing your own life. Pastors who are growing their lives create congregations of people who grow their lives in turn.

Pastors who have a hopeful view of life think kindly of themselves and others and have a sense of solid self-esteem. They create congregations that do the same with their own lives. In these congregations, we discover people who are advancing their own lives, building on their strengths, with a sense of confidence and a spirit of hope.

By contrast, pastors who live without much hope look down on themselves, think more poorly of themselves than they have a right to, and suffer from low self-esteem. They create congregations that do the same. It is not accidental that some congregations are this way. To be sure, people bring their own perceptions with them. Nevertheless, they then experience a series of pastors who live without much hope. It is no wonder some congregations suffer from a combination of low self-esteem, a sense of powerlessness, wishful thinking, and compulsion toward perfectionism, with the dual dilemmas of depression and dependency.

Healthy people claim the gift of hope God gives them. They do not look down on themselves, think more poorly of themselves than they have a right to, or suffer from low self-esteem. They develop solid self-esteem. They build their lives on the hope of God. They grow and develop their lives. The result is that they develop constructive relationships with those around them.

Who we are and who we are becoming is whom we create around us. People live the way they experience that others live. As people see how you live with hope, they gain clues for how they can live with hope. With integrity, be hopeful about your new beginning. Live a life of hope in your shepherding, preaching, leading, and sharing in the community. Have fun with your family. Grow the team. Live in hope. God bless and be with you.

# The Author

Kennon L. Callahan, Ph.D., author of many books, is best known for *Twelve Keys to an Effective Church*, which has formed the basis for the widely acclaimed movement of mission growth. His two recent books, *Twelve Keys for Living* and *Preaching Grace*, are useful companion books to *A New Beginning*.

# Index

219